The His

of

Chichester's Canal

by

Alan H. J. Green BSc CEng MICE

SUSSEX INDUSTRIAL
ARCHAEOLOGY SOCIETY

2005

Published by

SUSSEX INDUSTRIAL ARCHAEOLOGY SOCIETY

42 Falmer Avenue, Saltdean, Brighton, Sussex BN2 8FG

ISBN 0-9512036-1-4

Printed and bound by RPM Print & Design,
2-3 Spur Road, Quarry Lane, Chichester, Sussex PO19 8PR

CONTENTS

Acknowledgments

A work of this nature can only be produced with assistance and I owe thanks to a great many people in this respect. Writing acknowledgments carries a high risk of omitting someone so if I have committed this sin I crave pardon – it was certainly not deliberate!

Thanks have to start with the ever-helpful staff of those bodies who hold records relating to the Portsmouth and Arundel Navigation namely : West Sussex Record Office in Chichester, The National Library of Scotland in Edinburgh, The Institution of Civil Engineers in London, Portsmouth Record Office and Portsmouth City Library. To Rosemary Gilmour and Simon Kitchin of Chichester District Museum go thanks for their searching out photographs and advertisements for canal-basin traders.

To Chris Bryan, Adge Roberts, Andrew Berriman and Debra Wallace go thanks for their having made available their collections of canal-related material and to Linda Wilkinson and Jean Fitchew of the Chichester Ship Canal Trust for supplying information about the Canal Society. To Geoff Girling goes thanks for making available the lantern slides in the Outram Collection, one of which has been reproduced here, and to Doug Stephenson, the former British Railways Southern Region Parliamentary Assistant and John King of the Network Rail Records Section for advice regarding the construction of the Bognor branch.

To Adge Roberts goes a special vote of thanks for his agreeing to read and comment on the draft manuscript of this book, thus giving it the benefit of his encyclopaedic knowledge of the works on the Ford to Hunston section of the canal.

Finally to Richard Waterhouse at RPM Print & Design, my thanks for his patience in interpreting my complicated instructions in the production of the finished book.

INTRODUCTION

The Chichester Canal has always been a part of my life. As a young boy in the 1950s we used to visit a family friend, Miss Johnson, who lived at Fairhaven, a bungalow at the end of King's Avenue overlooking the canal. Fairhaven had a back gate which opened onto the tow path (for which privilege Miss Johnson was charged 2/6d per annum by the City Council), and this provided a scenic route to our destination and an opportunity to feed the swans and ducks. In the 1960s, when I attended Chichester High School for Boys, the tow path as far as Hunston, including Poyntz Bridge, formed part of the cross-country course which I traversed frequently. In the 1970s I moved to a house which overlooked the canal basin by which time I had embarked on a career of civil engineering in railways, a career which frequently involved me in the parliamentary process for authorising public works and contracts for building the same. By now the canal also offered engineering as well as local-history interest.

It was Linda Wilkinson of the Chichester Ship Canal Trust who first suggested that I write the history of the Sussex Line of the Portsmouth and Arundel Navigation, a waterway project which finally linked Chichester to the sea in 1822 and to the canal network in 1823.

It is generally well known that the Portsmouth and Arundel Navigation was a commercial failure but the reasons behind this– a catalogue of incompetence and ineptitude by the company, its contractors and its resident engineer – are probably less well known.

In this book the history of Chichester's canal, which can only be described as *extraordinary,* is told in detail. The task of researching it can only be described as having been a pleasure.

Chichester
November 2004

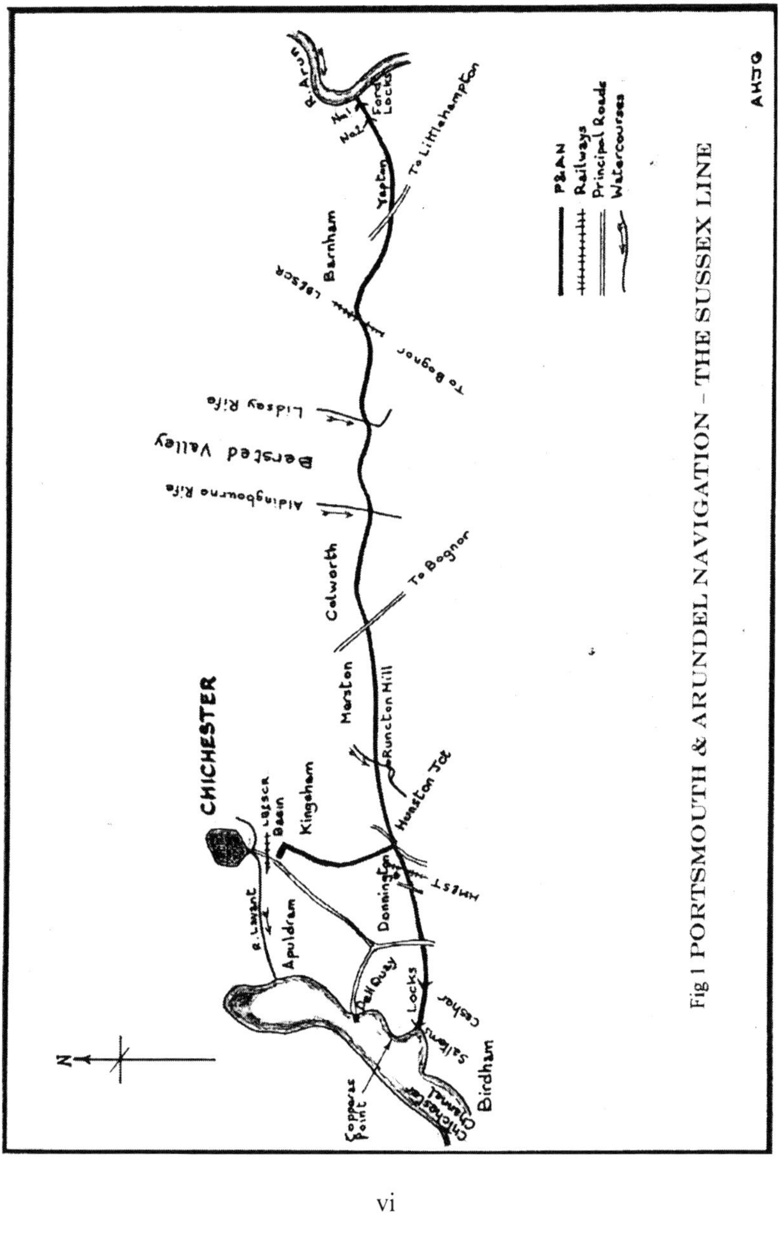

Fig 1 PORTSMOUTH & ARUNDEL NAVIGATION – THE SUSSEX LINE

CHAPTER I

Schemes that came to nought

Until the middle of the eighteenth century transporting bulky goods around the country was a slow and hazardous business. The options were horse-drawn wagon, coastal shipping or, where available, navigable river. Many journeys involved a combination of at least two of these modes with the attendant double handling, and the poor state of the roads resulted in frequent over-turnings of wagons and damage to goods.

In 1759 the highly successful Bridgewater Canal opened between Manchester and Worsley and this provided the impetus for the construction of a national canal network providing cheap and safe transport of goods across the country.

Chichester was, in the broadest sense of the word, a coastal town but its proximity to the sea was occasioned by its being at the head of an inland channel rather than hard at its side. The nearest landing point was at Dell Quay, nearly two miles away by indirect and rough roads and so it was not surprising that as early as 1585 a proposal was made to link the city to the harbour by canal and an Act of Parliament* was passed to permit its construction. Its heading stated its purpose as being *To bring to the haven of the City of Chichester by a new cut channel to the suburbs of the same,*

The preamble to the Act lists the drawbacks of trading via Dell Quay:- *The said key*[sic] *is about a mile and a halfe distant from the said city of Chichester and hath neither at it nor neare it, any houses or other places of receipte fit for the safe custody of wares, or the harbouring and refreshing of merchauntes &c.*

It then goes on to lament the inadequacy of the roads into the city centre and to impress upon Her Majesty the benefits that the

* 27 Eliz Cap xxii

proposed canal would bring. The canal was to be promoted by the Corporation but unfortunately it was never constructed.

In the Georgian period trade via Dell Quay was increasing and James Dallaway, writing in 1815,[1] gives some statistics for it:

Year	**Ships**	**Tons**	**Men**
1786	48	2128	143
1793	77	4085	273
1800	68	2771	186
1807	80	3043	213
1813	101	3602	337

He lists exports as being flour to Devonshire and Cornwall, timber to Portsmouth and Plymouth Dockyards and malt to Ireland whilst imports included barley from Norfolk, provisions from Ireland, coals from Newcastle, Spanish wool and wine from Portugal. What Dallaway excluded from his list was building materials which included softwood from Scandinavian countries, Purbeck stone paving from Poole and slate from Wales[2]. It was owing to the high cost of importing bulky building materials that local materials were preferred, so Georgian Chichester became a brick rather than a stone town. An additional problem for colliers was the need to transfer their cargoes onto barges at Itchenor as they were too large to sail up to Dell Quay[3] thus, with the final part of the journey into the city being by horse-drawn wagon, coals from Newcastle had to be triple-handled. Repairs to Dell Quay and its approach road were a constant drain on the Council's funds as is recorded in their minutes[4].

The idea of a canal was revived in 1801 when a Bill was prepared to make a cut from Southgate direct to the Harbour at Court Farm Barn, Birdham. The deposited plan[5] was drawn at a scale of 8 chains to the inch by J A Florance who signed and dated it *Chichester 1801*. Florance obviously could not decide how to terminate the canal at Southgate since the detailing at this end just peters out, but this idea would have provided a fairly direct and convenient route into the city. This scheme too came to nought but in 1802 the London and Portsmouth Canal Company was formed and on 14 October that year they published a printed resolution[6] to direct John Rennie to proceed with a survey of the route. The choice of Rennie was a wise one as he had become, alongside Thomas Telford, one of the leading civil engineers of his day. John Rennie (1761-1821) had been educated at Edinburgh University, whence he graduated in 1783, and set up business in London as a civil engineer quickly gaining a reputation as a man of skill and versatility. In London he built London[†] Southwark and Waterloo bridges whilst of his canal works the greatest achievement was the Kennet and Avon, running 57 miles from Newbury to the Avon at Bath and involving some 70 locks, five aqueducts and three tunnels. So much in demand was Rennie that his fees in 1810 were equivalent in today's terms to £1200 per day[7]! A vast deposited plan[8] for a canal, now in the collection at the West Sussex Record Office bears the title:-

PLAN
Of the Proposed
LONDON & PORTSMOUTH
CANAL
1802

The plan carries no signature but matches the description of a scheme by Rennie[9] for a circuitous, 100-mile route from the Croydon Canal to Arundel via Merstham, Crawley and Newbridge. The last section of the navigation was to be a canal leaving the Arun below Arundel and running inland to Portsmouth via Barnham and Oving, passing to the south of Chichester. This scheme, whilst it would have put Chichester on the canal network, would not have given access to the sea at Chichester Harbour so all sea-borne trade from the east would have had to have gone to Portsmouth and come back again along the new cut. There is an 1803 plan[10] for another version of this scheme[*] (which too is unsigned but again almost certainly Rennie's) also taking the canal past Chichester on an inland route to

---

[†] London Bridge was, of course, a rebuilding.

[*] Unfortunately this plan is now too frail to be examined but is described in Sussex Record Society Vol 66.

Portsmouth. Both proposals came to nought. On 22 March 1805 a meeting of The Common Council of the City of Chichester[11] was held which resolved *that an Engineer or some other proper person be employed to ascertain the practicability of bringing water either from the salt works at Appledram or from any other part of the arm of the sea up to the city, and that all expenses of the survey shall be paid for out of the funds of the Body.*

At first reading it seems that the Council were proposing, for some inexplicable reason, a scheme for piping seawater into the city but it was in fact another proposal for a canal. The person chosen to carry out the survey was John Rennie and he made his report[12] to the Mayor and Corporation on 22 July 1805. In it he starts by telling them what they already knew namely that Dell Quay (or *Del key* as he so quaintly put it) was inconvenient and then goes on to describe two options (*projects in contemplation*) for the Council's consideration. The surveys for these were carried out for Rennie by the same J A Florance who had devised the 1801 scheme. Both options came with the sub-options of either a sixteen foot or a thirteen foot depth. The first option was for *a ship canal* to run from Birdham (Salterns) via Donnington to Stockbridge, a distance of three and a half miles, estimated at £38,300 for the deep and £27,767 for the shallow versions. The second was for *a ship canal* to run from *the channel opposite Copperas Point along the shore near Appledram Sluice and from there pass up the vale of the Appledram Stream to the City, being a distance of two miles and a half.* This option weighed in at £31,733 for the deep and £22,970 for the shallow versions. This is the only time that the term *ship canal* was coined officially in respect of Chichester and it should be pointed out that either of these would have been very grand waterways worthy of the title; 90 feet wide in the case of the deep versions or 75 feet for the shallow.

Rennie points out in his report that his preference was for the Birdham-Stockbridge option since, despite its higher cost, it would be available for longer periods within the tide-cycle owing to the greater natural depth of the channel at Birdham. The report (described in the minutes as *a letter from John Rennie Esq*) was read to the Council at their meeting of 12 August 1805 and the plans (now missing) were considered producing the following resolution:

> *That as far as this Body are concerned they shall be willing to accede to one of such Plans by which it is projected that the course of the Water shall be brought up to the City shall be from Longmore Point in the Parish of Birdham thro:the Parish of Donnington provided that in the Adoption of such Plan the Quay Dues and Customs payable to the Body shall be secured in future.*

That proved to be the end of it. There were no resolutions either to proceed with or abandon the idea, and Rennie's 1805 schemes were consigned to the growing pile of unfulfilled ambitions.

Rennie was, however, to return to Chichester in 1810 when he revived and altered his 1803 scheme as a proposal for a *Grand Southern Canal* capable of carrying Thames barges to run from Tonbridge to Portsmouth[13]. Starting on the River Medway it would be routed to Horsham then down the Arun Valley to Arundel whence, once again, a canal would run westwards to Portsmouth via Chichester. The Chichester Common Council discussed this at their meeting of 25 June 1810[14] noting that a survey was shortly expected to be made on the south side of the city *relative to the projected Canal from Surry*[sic] *to Portsmouth.* They resolved to form a committee to consult with the surveyors regarding building a *barge canal* from Dell Quay *or any neighbouring part* to the city. Such was their faith in the Medway scheme that on 22 October they resolved to subscribe to five shares in the project. Unfortunately the Bill was defeated in its second reading by 100 votes to 17 owing to the powerful opposition of some influential landowners,[15] so yet another scheme was lost. We do not know whether the Council recovered its investment.

The next year, 1811, another proposal was made to provide a direct cut from Chichester to the Harbour, this time by William Nicholson a civil engineer who gave his address as *Bloomsbury Square, London.* The exquisitely-drawn plan[16] shews a canal starting at the mouth of the River Lavant (i.e north of Dell Quay) and running to a basin in Westgate. The cut was to be dead straight and, at about a mile in length with only three locks, would have been the cheapest option, but some heavy dredging of the channel would have been needed. It also crossed the River Lavant at two points but no detail of how this was to be achieved was given. In the hand-written book of reference, Nicholson refers to the 1585 scheme pointing out that his is a version of it but...*amending and rendering [it] more effectual an Act.* Needless to say this too came to nought but the Council had obviously not given up their quest for a canal since, at their meeting of 18 February 1813,[17] they resolved to pay a bill for £148 8s *due to Messrs Giles and Co for surveying and levelling a line of canal from the South Gate to the Salterns.* There is nothing about this survey having been commissioned or what happened to it but Netlam and Francis Giles, to give the creditors their proper title, did later carry out the survey for the Portsmouth and Arundel Navigation of which more anon. After eight aborted attempts Chichester was forced to wait another nine years to be served by a canal.

References Chapter I

[1] Dallaway, James A History of the Western Division of the County of Sussex Vol 1 1815, page 211

[2] Farrant J H The Seaborne trade of Sussex 1720-1845, Sussex Archaeological Collection, Vol.114, 1976

[3] WSRO Raper M292 Report of the Portsmouth and Arundel Canal sub-committee to subscribers May 1817

[4] WRSO C/3 Chichester Common Council Minute Book 1783-1828

[5] WSRO QDP/W2

[6] National Library of Scotland, Rennie Papers MS19782

[7] Chrimes, M British Civil Engineering Biography – Part 2 1790-1830 Proceedings of Institution of Civil Engineers No 157, August 2004 (Paper No 12637)

[8] WSRO QDP/W3

[9] Hadfield, Charles, The Canals of South and South East England 1969

[10] WSRO QDP/W4

[11] WRSO C/3 op cit

[12] Institution of Civil Engineers, Rennie Papers REN/RB/08/310-313

[13] Hadfield, Charles op cit

[14] WSRO C/3 op cit

[15] Hadfield, Charles op cit

[16] WSRO QDP/W24

[17] WSRO C/3 op cit

CHAPTER II

Birth of the Portsmouth & Arundel Navigation

Amongst the myriad Rennie papers is a collection relating to *the London and Portsmouth Canal*[1] commencing in 1802. It consists largely of correspondence and by 1817 the project references change to *The Portsmouth and Arun Canal* acknowledging that the greater project had been abandoned and Rennie was now working upon a *de minimis* version. The Wey and Arun Navigation* had opened in 1816 completing an inland route from London to Littlehampton so it only required one more heave to continue this on to Portsmouth. On 29 May 1817 the Committee of the Portsmouth and Arun Canal published[2] what was in effect an appeal for subscribers to this end headed :-

FACTS submitted by the Sub-Committee appointed for the purpose of conducting the Bill for the PORTSMOUTH and ARUN CANAL through Parliament to the Subscribers and Supporters of the same.

The Committee sounded a rallying cry with the words:-*The Committee offer the following statement, by which it will appear that a very extensive Trade must be carried on the intended Canal; and that the benefit to the holders of shares is certain.*

Unfortunately this assurance was to prove somewhat wide of the mark, as we shall see, but the Committee went on confidently predicting that some 6000 tons would be carried in the first year consisting of corn, grain, livestock, timber, coals, bricks, chalk and manure. They had done some homework regarding trade between London and Chichester and pointed out that *four waggons arrive from London at one house and two at each of other two houses, every week and return, and in the coasting trade there are three vessels of 100tons each and one of 70 tons... the aggregate number of their*

---

* For the history of that fascinating waterway see *London's lost route to the Sea* by PAL Vine David & Charles 1965

cargoes in the year 1816 was, from London, 18 and from Chichester to London 19.

The document went on to explain how coal traffic would benefit being as it presently cost 1/ 6d per chaldron* to convey it by barge from Itchenor to Dell Quay and then another 4/- per chaldron on top to convey it via the turnpike road into Chichester. The Canal Company would convey the coal all the way to the city for a mere 1/6 per ton! Setting out the rates for comparison using a mixture of volumetric and weight units was a little disingenuous as it suggested that the savings were better than they actually were (The old rate equated to 4/9d per ton in total) but it must have made convincing reading. The final claim was that through trade between London and Portsmouth was estimated to be *an important source of prosperity to the undertaking* as the average existing traffic over the two previous years had exceeded 20,000 tons.

A Bill, drafted by Atcheson and Greetham, was laid before Parliament in 1817 for : *Making and maintaining a Navigable Canal from the River Arun to Chichester Harbour and from thence to Langstone and Portsmouth Harbours with a Cut or Branch from Hunston Common to or near the City of Chichester, and for improving the Navigation of the Harbour of Langstone, and Channels of Langstone and Thorney.* The Bill[3] contained an engraved deposited plan which states that it was *Surveyed under the direction of JOHN RENNIE Esq, CE FRS &c &c by Netlam and Francis Giles†, New Inn, London 1815.*

The original plan from which the engraving was made is at West Sussex Record Office[4] and it carries a long section which was omitted from the engraved version. This plan depicts the scheme that was finally to bring a canal to Chichester. Rennie had submitted an earlier report to the Committee, dated 27 January 1816,[5] describing the works and giving an overall estimate of £118,990 for the scheme between Ford and Portsea, but at that stage the branch to Chichester

* A chaldron is a volumetric measure equal to 36 bushels

† Netlam and Francis Giles were brothers who regularly worked with Rennie as surveyors

was mentioned only as an "optional extra" and not included in the estimate!

Starting from the River Arun, by the Ship and Anchor Inn at Ford, the proposed canal would run in a westerly direction via Yapton, Barnham and Hunston to reach Chichester Harbour at Salterns near Birdham, a distance of 11 miles 75 chains, and from a junction at Hunston there was to be a branch, 1 mile 21 chains long, to Chichester terminating at a basin just below Southgate. Under this scheme Chichester would thus be connected both to the sea and to the canal network.

Beyond Birdham the waters of Chichester Harbour would be used to pass across the top of Thorney and Hayling Islands to Langstone Harbour whence another canal would be constructed across the bottom of Portsea Island to serve a basin at the picturesquely-named Halfway Houses. In this book we will not concern ourselves with the Navigation beyond Hunston but be very parochial and concentrate on the canal in Sussex and its all-important branch to Chichester.

The Bill received Royal Assent on 7 July 1817 (apparently after a smooth passage through the house since only a small number of changes were made to its wording) to become Portsmouth and Arundel Navigation Act*. The Chichester Common Council had got wind of it however, and on 11 February 1817[6] they expressed their concern that in the progress of the Bill care should be taken to protect the dues and customs payable to the Council as *it is not exactly known what the projectors of this Bill mean to do for this purpose.* Alderman John Newland (a solicitor) was charged with communicating with the promoters and reporting back to the Council. The results of Alderman Newland's communications are not recorded† but both the Bill and the Act made protection provisions in respect of the Council's dues.

---

* 57 Geo III Cap 63

† The Common Council minutes are invariably tantalisingly brief – one has to question whether the clerk might have been asleep most of the time!

Unusually, in the individual printed copies of the Act the sections are not numbered and, as it runs to 110 pages, locating and cross referring specific issues is made very difficult. It was only in the edition printed for inclusion in the Statute Book that the sections were numbered so, where I have quoted section numbers, they refer to that edition[†]. Much of the wording is fairly standard for a canal act and it sets out, inter alia, the way in which the funds were to be raised, the procedure for land acquisition, the dimensions of the cut, the tolls which will be applied and the way the venture would be managed. Curiously, no individual accommodation or occupation works are specified in the Act; in the case of bridges it was left to the Company to provide as many as were needed for the use of occupiers of land, but subject to a judicial ruling in the event of a dispute arising.

No fewer than 304 promoters are listed in the Act including the Duke of Norfolk, the Earl of Egremont, and a Captain John Bligh RN(!) Sadly this was not the Captain Bligh of mutiny on the Bounty fame as his name was, of course, Thomas.

The Company was empowered to raise up to £126,000 by the issue of 2,520 equal shares and, in the event of that proving insufficient, they were allowed to raise a further £10,000, subject to a resolution at a special meeting, by share issue or mortgage. The Act required the Company's affairs to be handled by a Committee of Management who should hold annual general meetings at Portsmouth Town Hall on the third Tuesday of May *at eleven of the clock in the forenoon* - even the conduct of the Committee was prescribed! These meetings were indeed held in the early years and printed reports were produced for them from which we learn much about the construction and opening of the canal and also the financial problems which set in at such an early stage. In these reports the Portsmouth and Arundel Company seemingly could not decide whether it was running a *Navigation* or a *Canal* as both terms are used in its company title[*].

[†] There is a copy of this version in Portsmouth City Record Office

[*] The Act used the term *Navigation*

The Committee of Management produced a printed *Address* on 5 August 1817[7] which reported to shareholders that Royal Assent had been given to the Bill *on the 7th ultimo* and gave the following confident statement about the costs:

The Survey for this undertaking was made under the direction of Mr RENNIE, through a line of country so peculiarly eligible, that no Locks were found to be requisite except at the extremities, and therefore 124,452l appear by the Estimate to be all that is necessary to carry it into effect; but insomuch as great reductions have taken place in the prices of Land, Labour and Materials, since Mr RENNIE made the said estimate, it is beyond a doubt that the above sum is greater than will be required, and the Committee feel warranted in this conclusion, because certain opulent Persons have expressed a willingness to undertake the execution of the measure, at an abatement of 10l per cent on the aforesaid estimated amount.

The haphazard use made in the report of mid-sentence capital letters is characteristically Georgian, but such was their pride in having secured the services of John Rennie the Committee obviously felt it necessary to print his whole name in capitals every time it appeared. The address went on to confirm that £101,250 - five-sixths of the required sum - had been subscribed prior to the passing of the Act and the £50 shares could be bought by instalments of £5 payable every three months. It also bravely (or perhaps rashly) predicted that the annual revenue would be £21,150-16s-0d.

The dimensions of the canal were stipulated by Section V of the Act not to exceed 26 yards breadth and six feet in depth but the 26 yards was not the width of the waterway per se but the maximum permitted land-take and so included for the tow paths and earthworks. However where the level of the canal went more than six feet above or below virgin ground level and/or wharfs or passing places were needed the land take could go up locally to 70 feet. All this must have been rather unsettling for landowners who could not be certain how much they would lose and it is interesting to note that the deposited plans of the railway age were to shew the centre line of the work flanked by "limits of deviation" which required the promoters to have carried out some preliminary design of earthworks in order to determine the required land take at Bill stage.

When construction commenced in 1818 (see Chapter III) it was in compliance with these requirements of the Act, however very soon representations were made by the Corporation and others[8] for the canal to be enlarged between Birdham and Chichester to enable vessels of 100tons to be accommodated. As this would entail a depth in excess of the six feet stipulated in the Act a further Bill was prepared to legislate for it and at the same time empower the construction of a new road between the canal basin and the city[*]. To pay for this extra construction work - estimated at £7000 - the tolls over the enlarged sections of the canal needed to be increased and provision for this was also included in the Bill. This Bill achieved Royal Assent on 21 June 1819[†] and the resultant Act ran to 33 sections – numbered properly this time –incorporating all the above.

The Act was headed *An Act for giving further powers to the Company of Proprietors of the Portsmouth and Arundel Navigation, and to the Company of Proprietors of the Wey and Arun Canal, and to confirm an Agreement entered into between the said companies.* The "agreement" referred to was one between the two Companies about charging lesser tolls for through traffic passing over the two systems than those stipulated by the 1817 Act.

The deposited plan[9] was drawn by James Hollinsworth and is signed and dated *Chichester, 29 September 1818*. It is rather scratchy in its draughtsmanship and shews the Chichester Branch and the main line west of Hunston together with an enlarged detail of the proposed road which was to lead from the north side of the basin to Southgate. Originally known as Canal Road it was later to become the public highway called Basin Road.

James Hollinsworth had been appointed Resident Engineer to the project by John Rennie at a salary[10] of £500 per annum. This was an

---

[*] The Bill also provided for additional works at the Portsmouth end to accommodate 150 ton vessels

[†] 59 Geo III Cap 104

important position as he was to be Rennies' eyes and ears in overseeing the contractors, ensuring that the work was carried out in accordance with the Engineer's specifications and sorting out the inevitable day-to-day problems that arose. Hollinsworth had been involved with Rennie on many projects since 1796 including the construction of the Crinan Canal[11] and had acted for him, between 1811 and 1817, as Resident Engineer on the construction of Waterloo Bridge in London. The Rennie Papers relating to the Waterloo Bridge scheme[12] indicate that considerable powers had been delegated to Hollinsworth; in addition to the day-to-day administration of the contract he had calculated for Rennie the time needed to construct an arch, agreed all quantities with the contractors and made regular progress reports to Rennie who was the Engineer. In view of Rennie's staggering workload having a trusted representative on site was essential since although Rennie managed to cram so much into his days even he was unable to be in more than one place at once!

The fact that Hollinsworth had been entrusted with the production of the deposited plan for the second Bill is another demonstration of Rennie's reliance upon him and when the great man died in 1821 Hollinsworth took over full responsibility for the completion of the works. During his time at Chichester Hollinsworth and his family lived at Rumboldswhyke[13], for which he was paid an annual allowance of £50 but so far it has not been possible to identify the house he occupied.

One of the greatest problems facing the promoters of new public works can be that of concluding land-purchase agreements but this activity appears from the reports to have passed off fairly smoothly for, by the general meeting of 18 May 1819, it was reported[14] that the negotiations had been concluded on satisfactory terms save for *one now absent in France...who possesses but a single Field that interferes with the line.* This absentee was William Dearling, a colourful entrepreneur who had a stake in many ventures in and around Chichester and had fled to France in 1817[15] leaving his shaky financial affairs in the hands of a trust. The parcel of land concerned was at Donnington. However, despite this bold statement by the

Company, it is clear that *satisfactory conclusion* was far from the case for, as we shall see in the next chapter, when the Contractor submitted a substantial claim he cited difficulties in gaining possession of certain lands on the Ford to Hunston stretch.

A major landowner affected by the canal was Major General John Gustavus Crosbie, of Northlands in Funtington, whose holdings fully matched the splendour of his name. He had married Frances White Thomas, heiress to the Page family fortune[16], in 1802 and thereby added lands in Chichester, Donnington and Barnham (including Barnham Court) to his family estate. He had also so acquired Donnington Manor but there is no record that he ever lived in it for up to 1811 he leased it to the said William Dearling, with whom he was then associated in the Newtown development[17].

Fig 2 Portrait bust of Major General John Gustavus Crosbie, in Donnington Church. His landholdings in the area were affected by the construction of the Portsmouth & Arundel Navigation and the swing bridge in Donnington was named after him.
(Author, courtesy of St Georges PCC)

Crosbie was not a promoter[*] of the Portsmouth and Arundel Canal but, despite this, the swing bridge carrying the road over the canal at Donnington was named after him; perhaps the size of his affected landholding and the amicable way in which he released it earned him the respect of the Company. Just down the road from Crosbie Bridge is Donnington Church where many of the Crosbies, including Major General John Gustavus himself, are buried. He is commemorated there by a splendid portrait bust, the sculptor of which is unknown.

A third Act of Parliament relating to this scheme was passed in 1821,[†] principally giving powers to the River Arun Navigation Company to carry out works to permit the passage of boats drawing 3 feet I inch, but also confirming certain agreements made between the Arun Navigation and Portsmouth and Arundel Navigation Companies regarding through traffic over the completed link to London. In the event of the Arun Company not completing these improvement works within three months, the Act gave powers to the Portsmouth and Arundel Company to take over the Arun works, complete them themselves, and recover their costs.

References Chapter II

[1] National Library of Scotland MS19782
[2] WSRO Raper M292
[3] WRSO Fuller F/Lib21, a printed copy of the Bill
[4] WSRO QDP/W34
[5] Institution of Civil Engineers Rennie Papers REN/RB/8/310-313
[6] WSRO C/3 Chichester Common Council Minute Book 1783-1836
[7] WSRO Raper M293
[8] WSRO Raper M299 Report of Committee of Management 18 May 1819
[9] WSRO QDP/W38
[10] WSRO Raper M298 Notice to shareholders 4 August 1818

[*] At least not at the outset, for he is not so listed in the 1817 Act; however he may have become so later.

[†] 1&2 Geo IV Cap. lxii - enacted 28 May 1821

---

[11] Chrimes, M, Skempton Sir A (and others) Biographical Dictionary of Civil Engineers in Great Britain and Ireland 1500-1830, Thomas Telford 2002
[12] National Library of Scotland MS19776
[13] Chrimes. M, Skepton, Sir A (et al) op cit
[14] WSRO Raper 299 op sit
[15] Green, Alan H J. St John's Chapel and the New Town Chichester, Phillimore 2005
[16] ibid
[17] ibid

CHAPTER III

Building the Canal 1818-1823

In May 1818 tenders for constructing the canal were invited in the local papers and one Chichester builder who was unsuccessful was William Brooks. His lack of success was not on account of the magnitude of his tender but because he was late in submitting the same as a letter[1] from the Company Clerk to Brooks, dated 29 June 1818, reveals:

> *I have received your letter this morning and am sorry your application to me was not made before – as it will now be too late for you to avail yourself of any information I can give you. The fact is the Works have been advertised in several newspapers for six weeks to be let by public tender and all offers are required to be sent in by 11 o'clock on Wednesday night when the Committee will meet to decide on these - The specifications have been laying in this office for some time past for public inspection.*

Despite Mr J Williams, the Company Clerk, begging to remain Brooks' most obedient servant, Brooks would have been an unhappy man. He had been a contractor for several public buildings in Chichester including the Market House and St John's Chapel,[2] so the canal would have been the jewel in his crown; however he only had himself to blame since as a promoter of the canal project he should have had sufficient inside information about the tender dates! This was not to be the only admonishing letter Brooks would receive from the Canal Company as we shall see later.

The successful tender was that of Thomas Dyson and Thomas Thornton[*] with whom the Company entered into a contract on 4 August 1818[3] to construct the whole of the works, including those in

---

[*] Their address in correspondence is given as *Chichester* but neither Dyson nor Thornton were local contractors.

the Harbour and on Portsea Island, within two years and six months. Their tender sum was £64,050 which, when the cost of land purchase, legal expenses and contingencies for extras were added, gave a scheme total of £106,656 - well within Rennie's estimate. Work started straight away with the cutting of the ceremonial first sod at Ford on 20 August by the said Clerk, Mr J Williams,[4] and detailed accounts of the progress of the works are given in the Committee of Management's annual reports between 1818 and 1823[5].

Main Line -Ford to Hunston

At Ford two locks were constructed to lift vessels to Rennie's designed water level which was to be 12 feet above the off-spring high water mark[6] in the River Arun. The relatively flat coastal plain was not going to provide Rennie with much in the way of engineering challenges but as the only other locks were to be at Birdham, nearly 12 miles distant, the determination of this water level was critical. Rennie, from his survey, would have known the levels of the existing watercourses to be crossed and have carried out mass haul calculations to balance the amount of material excavated with that required for embankments so as to minimise the need to import or export any spoil. Spoil movement, as we shall see, gave rise to a major contractual claim but the Act had catered for the eventuality of an excess of excavated material by permitting it to be spread on adjacent land provided it was covered with nine inches of indigenous topsoil.

Also at Ford was an engine house accommodating the 40 hp steam pump that was to raise water from the River Arun at the rate of 5000 gallons/minute to feed the east end of the cut. Now the fact that the River Arun was tidal at this point gave a high risk of salt water being introduced into the canal with consequential dire effects upon the local ecology. The Bill had obviously been petitioned over this by concerned landowners for a clause was added to the Act (Section LVI) stipulating rather picturesquely that the water could only be abstracted ... *not less than two hours after high water and from there until not exceeding one hour after flood... in order to prevent the water of said intended canals and cuts from becoming putrid and stagnant and thereby noxious to health.* Sinking the well was described as *a tedious operation* owing to encountering several springs but it was completed and the engine was steamed for the first time on 20 August 1819 to begin filling sections of the canal. In this it was kept going almost full time owing to leakage but soon a stream was discovered at Merston, described as *...having run copiously throughout the last Summer notwithstanding the great drought*, which was suitable for use as an auxiliary feed.

Two cottages were provided at Ford for the use of the lock keeper and the keeper of the engine. Happily these cottages survive but of the magnificent engine house there is no trace

Anyone travelling by train between Chichester and Barnham would be hard pressed to believe that they had crossed over two valleys, but they have; those at Bersted and Barnham that gave rise to the heaviest earthworks on the canal's main line, and whose construction was to cause an embarrassing delay to the opening of the Navigation. At Lidsey there was what was grandly referred to as "an aqueduct" to carry the canal over the Lidsey Rife. This structure was in fact a circular culvert, 10 feet in diameter, through a high embankment, so although an aqueduct in the strictest sense of the word it was hardly going to rival Telford's creation at Pontcysyllte! There was another aqueduct crossing the Aldingbourne Rife, this time of two eight-foot spans, plus a number of culverts to accommodate various other water courses. Sections of the canal were filled as excavation progressed so as to enable as much spoil as possible to be boated to the site of the Barnham Valley embankment, but this was not always without difficulty as many references in the reports to boating, such as this in 1820,[7] bears out *"... the water from the Engine did not reach Yapton for the purpose of boating until the 18th day of March last, and then, owing to some imperfection in the drain, the boats did not proceed to work regularly for three or four days.*

On the main line between Ford and Hunston 17 brick arch bridges were built for highway and accommodation purposes, the largest of these being at Yapton where the canal passed under the main road on a high skew. The secret of building skew arches was discovered by the Romans and it called for a high degree of skill; a skill which the contractors for the Portsmouth and Arundel Navigation signally lacked. The quality of brickwork in the two surviving brick arches in Yapton (Tack Lee and Burndell) reveals that the bricklayer did not have a clue how to turn an arch - even on so moderate a skew as these two possess - so how he coped at the main road (long since demolished) we can only guess. The bricks used in these works were all made on site using the abundant supplies of clay and brickearths; the report for May 1819 stated that *...Bricks are now in making in large quantities at six different parts of the canal...*

There were also seven cast-iron swing bridges (referred to as *swivel bridges*) between Ford and Hunston but these were only for accommodation/occupation purposes. Quite why, when masted vessels could not use this line, swing bridges were built at these locations rather than cheaper brick arches seems curious, but there is a possible clue to this mystery in the aforementioned contractors' claim which will be dealt with in Chapter IV. The swing bridges were all named after promoters and supporters of the project, one at Barnham being named *Hollinsworth Bridge.* There is a James Hollingsworth– spelt with a 'g' – in the list of promoters in the 1817 Act but whether this was a misspelling of our Resident Engineer (who signed his name without the 'g') or some other person* we cannot be absolutely certain. We will look at the construction of the bridges when we come to the Chichester Branch where one has survived

As we have seen in Chapter two, the Act of 1819 permitted the depth of the canal between Birdham and Hunston, and also on the Chichester branch, to be increased to take 100ton sailing vessels, but the Ford to Hunston section remained in accordance with the 1817 Act, having a depth of 4 feet 6inches and widths of 19 feet 6 inches at the bottom and 33 feet at the top[8] and was thus only capable of taking 75 ton horse-drawn barges.

---

* Interestingly most of the Committee of Management reports were printed by a Mr *Hollingsworth* – again with a 'g'- of Portsmouth.

Main Line - Hunston to Birdham

Hunston, 8 miles 78 chains from Ford, was the junction for the branch to Chichester and also the commencement of the enlarged section onwards to the sea at Birdham. From hereon the top width of the waterway was 46 feet 8 inches, with a depth of eight feet and there were no brick arches; all five crossings being made by cast-iron swing bridges so as to permit the passage of masted vessels. These bridges, once again, were named after promoters and supporters being from east to west: Crosbie, Cutfield, Dudley, Casher and Egremont. Crosbie and Cutfield bridges carried the Donnington and Birdham roads respectively but the others were either accommodation or occupation* works.

Fig 3. An etching by I J Wilson c1890 of Hunston Junction looking east. The brick arch carried the Selsey road over the main line. This was the last brick arch; all crossings beyond here to the sea being made with swing bridges. (WSRO)

* Accommodation bridges were provided to link lands that had been severed by the new works: occupation bridges were provided to maintain a private right of way across the new works.

The sea was entered at Birdham by two locks, for the outer one of which Rennie's lengthy and highly-detailed specification[9] exists. The lock was to be 76 feet long and 18 foot 6 inches wide at the copings and provided with a brick invert, for which the following extract from the specification demonstrates Rennie's attention to detail:

> *The bottom is to be an Inverted Arch of Brickwork 18 inches thick in the middle and increasing at the Side Walls, the Curves of which are to join in with it and the whole is to be laid on a good foundation Cut to its shape or puddle as the case might require. At the lower end of this Inverted Arch is to be a Fir or Elm Cill 30 feet long by 15 inches square having a row of 6 inch grooved sheeting piles driven to the depth of at least 15 feet, but as much deeper as the case may require and there is to be a puddle in front to connect with the solid ground below.*

The lower gates were to be founded on two rows of timber piles (beech or elm) each side driven into the sea bed whilst the gates themselves were to be *all of oak except the planking.* Rennie also prescribes the mixture for the lime mortar and specifies the bricks and stonework, the latter being either Bramley Fall or Cornish or Devonshire granite. Unfortunately the drawings referenced in Rennie's text have been lost, but with the tightness of his specification not much was left to the contractor's imagination. It requires the workmanship to be *to the entire satisfaction of the Resident Engineer* and doubtless this was the case with those brick arches* between Ford and Hunston, so it is of no credit to James Hollinsworth that he accepted such poor workmanship on behalf of his master. In the annual report for May 1820 progress at Birdham was described as *One sea lock at Chichester Harbour half built...* but two years later they were complete save for *a little clearing out of the outfall.*

The lower lock was known as Salterns, after the saltpans that occupied this part of the harbour, whilst the upper one was known

---

* The brickwork on the abutments of the swing bridges also left much to be desired. At Hollinsworth Bridge many the vertical joints are directly above each other!

variously as Casher or Manhood. Edward Casher, from whom the name derives, was a Portsmouth wine merchant and one of the original shareholders; he later became mayor of Portsmouth[10] and by 1830 was named in the reports as the chairman of the Committee of Management.

Cottages were provided for the use of each of the lock keepers and on the deposited plans for the 1817 Act[11] is indicated a work which was not implemented - another engine house. This feature is strange since the aforementioned Section LVI of the Act, forbidding pollution of the canal with seawater, carried wording to the effect that the canal ... *shall not be supplied with any water out of the said harbour of Chichester.* Fortunately for the promoters it was not found to be necessary to pump here owing to the springs found at Stockbridge[12], so no unlawful work was constructed*.

The Chichester Branch

Fig 4. The superstructure from Poyntz Bridge restored by Sussex Industrial Archaelolgy Society and relocated at Padwick Bridge near Chichester basin. (Author)

* The promoters did get into serious trouble over this at Portsmouth however where the Portsea Canal was fed with seawater which polluted nearby wells.

The branch to Chichester, which left the main line at Hunston Junction, was began in 1819 and again all crossings were made by cast-iron swing bridges. The first of these, and the only one to survive*, was Poyntz Bridge, named after William Poyntz MP, which enabled the tow path to cross over just beyond the junction. The abutments are of brick with stone copings and curved in plan having a clear opening between them of 20 feet. The abutment remote from the tow path carries a stone pivot block into which is set the lower half of a cast-iron ball race upon which the superstructure swung. The arrangement of this last can best be demonstrated at Casher Bridge at Birdham where, although the superstructure has long since gone, the pivot block, ball race and transom girders have survived as pictured in Fig 5 below.

Fig 5. The pivot block and transom girders of Casher Bridge at Birdham, which escaped destruction when the rest of the iron-work was removed. It has been raised on blocks to reveal the ball race. (Author, courtesy Chris Bryan and Adge Roberts)

The superstructure consists of four cast-iron girders of overall length 40 feet 7 inches (12.37m), supported at roughly the two-thirds point by two cast iron under-slung transoms, to which is bolted the

* Poyntz Bridge has since been rebuilt as a fixed structure but the old superstructure was removed and re-erected at Padwick bridge by Sussex Industrial Archaeological Society – See Chapter VI

upper half of the ball race. The swing bridge is balanced* by cast-iron counter weights slung beneath its short end, and the whole is finished with a timber deck and slender wrought-iron handrails. When open to canal traffic, no portion of the superstructure overhangs the waterway. All the bridges between Chichester and Birdham were identical to Poyntz bridge; those on the main line between Ford and Hunston were similar but as there was only a 14-foot clear opening they had shorter girders†. The ironwork was all made in 1820 by C&H Tickell of Southampton whose name, along with that of the bridge, was carried on the outer girders. Curiously, the Committee of Management reports, whilst carrying details of the progress with the construction of the abutments, make no mention of the casting and fabrication of the superstructures for any of the swing bridges.

The Chichester Branch headed off in a roughly north-north easterly direction from Hunston Junction passing through a long cutting below Stockbridge before curving to approach the basin situated to the south of the City. Just before the basin was an accommodation swing bridge named Padwick after a Hayling and Thorney Islands landowner. The basin was the only major engineering feature on the branch but, for some inexplicable reason, its construction was not included in the contract so it had to be built as a costly extra thereto. The canal entered the basin at its south-east corner requiring incoming vessels to make a sharp turn to port on arrival. The May 1819 Report of the Committee of Management[13] cites the progress being made at the basin :

> *The greatest part of the scite* [sic] *of the Basin and Wharfs, near Chichester, has been excavated to the level of the Wharfs, a depth of nearly eight feet below the natural surface of the ground; further progress cannot be made in this part until such time as a drain, which is now excavating, can be brought up to carry off the*

---

* As restored in its new location it is so finely balanced that the author's eight-year old (Australian) great nephew was able to start its 13-ton mass from rest with ease.

† Some buried remains of superstructures on the Ford- Hunston section have been recovered – see Chapter VI

water. The Road from the Basin to the Southgate in the City of Chichester is fenced off, and for the greatest part formed, and a Brick Arch has been turned over the River Lavant.

What the Committee did not mention was the fact that the banks on the Branch had had to be repaired by the contractors[14] following their having been *riotously destroyed...* by persons unknown.

The water that was hampering construction of the basin later became an asset when it, and another source encountered at Padwick Bridge,* provided a constant supply of water to the canal thus avoiding the need for a further pumping installation.

The road being constructed was of course Canal Road, authorised by the 1819 Act (later to become Basin Road) which ran due north from the east end of the basin and, after crossing the River Lavant, (then not culverted) turned west to join Southgate opposite the Fountain Inn. This involved the purchase and demolition of some properties belonging to the Corporation who had resolved[15] at their meeting of 17 January 1820 to charge the Canal Company £250 for the interest therein.

The basin was 400 by 115 feet (122 by 35 m) and the not-inconsiderable volume of excavated spoil (15,000 cubic yards) was boated five miles to the Bersted valley to build the embankment whose construction by May 1822 was falling hopelessly behind programme. During the excavation of the basin Roman remains were found including a hoard of 300 denarii in an earthenware pot[16].

Brick wharfs with stone copings were provided on all four sides of the basin and a warehouse at the east end, whilst at the end of the new road two flint double-fronted houses were built by the Canal Company, one of which is believed to have served as the Custom House[17].

A requirement of the Act (Section CXXVIII) was that milestones or mileposts should be provided every half mile. This was a statutory requirement on turnpike roads since milestones were useful not only for telling travellers where they were but for enabling the precise

---

* This spring was diverted into a cast-iron pipe which was taken below the canal bed level via an inverted siphon which fed upwards into the middle of the canal. It is still there.

location of necessary repairs to be reported. There is no evidence that these were ever provided on any of the arms of the Sussex line –or if they were all have mysteriously disappeared!

Fig 6. A view towards the canal basin from Padwick Bridge. The building on the right is a warehouse whilst ahead, on the opposite bank, can be seen the pair of houses on the corners of Basin Road. The tall chimney is to the gasworks retort house The Edwardian boy is probably getting ready to fish – this was a favourite spot for anglers.
(Chichester District Museum/Beaver Photography)

Having arrived at Chichester it is now appropriate to consider one prominent citizen, namely John Marsh, who surprisingly was not a proprietor of the canal project. Marsh (1752-1828) was a barrister by profession who moved to Chichester in 1787, living at 8 North Pallant where he remained until his death. His estates in Kent yielded some £1100 per annum which enabled him to live the life of a country gentleman and pursue his passions of composing, playing the organ and viola, astronomy, writing and mathematics. He was director of the Band of the Sussex Militia and organised subscription concerts at the Assembly Rooms. John Marsh was a great philanthropist and also an investor in most Chichester ventures including the Lancastrian Schools, St John's Chapel, the Theatre, and the Infirmary. Given this, and his passion for technology, it is thus odd that he chose not to invest in the Portsmouth and Arundel Navigation unless of course his keen business sense warned him that it was doomed to failure! Marsh was also a prolific diarist and recorded his observations of Georgian Chichester, including the construction and opening of the canal, in his *Journal of my Private Life** His canal observations began on 9 February 1819 when he records[18]:-

> *There having been for sometime a Canal making from the River Arun to Dell Quay & a branch cutting from it to Chichester, I the next morning took a walk to see it with my brother who had been 2 or 3 times before to see it; the cut from the canal extending now to within about half a mile of Kingsham Farm.*

He had been on his travels in December 1821 and hence missed the major event of filling the basin, but on 29 January 1822 he refers to it:

> *The next morning I went to look at the bason* [sic] *at the head of the new cut to Chichester, into which the water had been let at Christmas and where now 2 vessels were building which I for the first time saw.*

Contractual problems

The Committee of Management reports generally gave a positive and reassuring message to the shareholders but the first hints that all might not be well came in that for May 1821 in respect of overcoming delays to the Works :

* The manuscripts for these are in the Huntingdon Museum in America but fortunately are available on microfilm at West Sussex Record Office. An edited edition of the journals down to 1801, by Brian Robins was published in 1998 by the Pendragon Press

> *... the Contractors (in consequence of communications had with them)have adopted a more energetic mode of carrying on the Company's Works by offering certain sums, in the way of bonus, to the different Sub-Contractors under them, provided such parts thereof as they have respectively engaged to perform be finished at specific periods. This stimulus has produced the effect of having double sets of men who work by night as well as by day, and it is hoped that the Portsea Line will be finished by about Michaelmas next and the whole line in about 40 weeks from this time.*

Quite how these extra men managed to work effectively on non-moonlit nights was left to the shareholders' imaginations, as was the means of funding the cost of the extra shifts. Unfortunately the 40-week aspiration was not to be achieved since one year later, although the section between Birdham and Chichester was reported as having opened, the works on the rest of the Sussex line were stated as requiring *a considerable time to complete,* citing the Barnham and Bersted embankments and the ground conditions there as being the particular problem. At Barnham a further 25,000 cubic yards needed to be boated in from the cutting at Ford whilst the embankment at Bersted required 16,000 cubic yards to come both from a stockpile at Donnington and the Canal Basin at Chichester. In linear terms outstanding works were 800 yards of excavation at Ford, plus 300 yards of embankment at Barnham Valley, and a further 100yds of the same at the Bersted Valley. With all these problems to be overcome the Committee could not foresee completion until December 1822 but by the meeting of 20 May 1823 the Ford to Hunston section was *still* not open; however the Committee were able to report that the contractor had named 26 May 1823 as the day *when your said Navigation will be ready.*

Whilst these reports regale shareholders with the Herculean efforts being made by the Committee to get the Navigation open as quickly as possible, they make no illusions to the underlying causes of the delay or (naturally) their part in it. For their part the Contractors were putting together a substantial claim containing some amazing allegations about the Company and its Resident Engineer which we shall come to later.

Open at last

As a result of the delays outlined above the Portsmouth and Arundel Navigation was subject to two official openings and, in true Georgian style, both were marked with a bun-fight. On 9 April 1822 the section between Birdham and Chichester Basin was declared open and John Marsh, now aged 70, attended as he records in his Journal[19];

> *On the following day the Cut from the new canal from the Arun to Chich'r Harbour up to the basin at Chichester was opened which caused a great concourse of people to assemble, & in the afternoon some vessels came up from Portsmouth, Itchenor &c – As there was a cold easterly wind tho' at times a clear sky, I just walked down once about 3 o'clock when, finding it very uncertain at what time the vessels wo'd arrive, I returned home being fearful of renewing my cough which had considerably abated*[*]*. – As however in the evening I drank tea at my Son's I there had a full account of the operation of the afternoon from my grandsons who came up to the basin with other company in Mr Johnson's pleasure boat which was followed by 3 others with a band of music so that altogether with the amazing concourse of spectators it appeared to have been a very gay scene. Afterwards there was a grand dinner at the Dolphin at a guinea a head to which the Duke (who with the Duchess had been at the Canal) had sent a buck.*

Marsh was blissfully unaware that the cause of the uncertainty about the arrival time of the vessels was the procession from Portsmouth, towed by the Company's steam tug *Egremont,* having run aground in the Emsworth Channel[20]. It never did turn up so what the rest of the Marsh contingent witnessed was the unofficial procession of hangers-on!

Marsh had earlier recorded two vessels that were being built at the basin and he duly witnessed the launch of them. On 18 April

---

[*] Seventy was an extraordinary age for a Georgian so one can forgive Marsh's insistence on nursing his health!

Richmond was launched by the eponymous Duke in the presence of the Duchess and *a great multitude of spectators of whom I made one.* The second was launched on 14 June and sounds a most curious craft; *...the Selsey, made out of the wreck of a Vessel on that coast, was launched at the Chichester Basin, in the presence of a large concourse of spectators of whom I made one.* F D Heneghan[21] quotes another account, this time by "an elderly Cicestrian", which says that the two vessels were brigs and that the second was called *Chichester* rather than Selsey and also that they never returned to the basin as they were too large to do so with a cargo.

The second opening – to mark the completion of the whole project this time – took place more than a year later, on the 26 May 1823, and the Committee posted an invitation in the press[22] to all *Subscribers and Friends of the Undertaking* to attend the event, pointing out that barges would be available at eleven o'clock to convey them from Ford to Chichester where a dinner would be provided at the Swan Inn[†]. The following day they would re-embark at half past nine for Chichester Harbour whence they would be towed by the Company's Steam Vessel, The *Egremont*, to Portsmouth where another dinner would be provided. The day was obviously no-less grand than the first opening, John Marsh duly attended, albeit only as an observer, and was obviously impressed:

On Monday ye 26th the new Canal, which last year was opened from Chichester to Dell Quay, was now opened to the River Arun so that there was now a direct inland communication from Chichester to London & also to Littlehampton. On this occasion several vessels came up to the Basin at Chichester amongst which was the Richmond launched there last year & a large concourse of people was attracted, it being celebrated with music playing, colours flying and guns firing, the whole concluding with a public diner at The Swan.

[†] The Swan was a coaching inn near the Cross in East Street, much used for ceremonial feasting. It closed when the arrival of the railway deprived it of business.

Once again the two accounts of the vessels launched from the basin differ – here Marsh categorically says that The *Richmond* did come back! What Marsh did not record was the number of vessels leaving Ford which *The Sussex Weekly Advertiser,* in its issue of 2 June, reported as comprising the Earl of Egremont's pleasure barge, the barges of the mayors of Arundel and Guildford followed by eight goods barges which had previously arrived at the canal. At Hunston an 80-ton schooner and five sloops joined the procession up to the basin. The *Brighton Gazette's* report of 5 June adds that the procession was nearly a mile long and that the bands were those of the Sussex Militia plus private ones from Arundel.

The canal was at last fully open but the contractual arguments were coming to a head.

Cash flows and ebbs

I suspect most readers' eyes will glaze over at the presentation of financial statistics (mine invariably do) but some investigation of the Company's financial positions, declared in their reports to the annual general meetings, is of help in understanding the contractual claim which we will come to next.

The financial reportings were brief, consisting only of statements about how much money had been received and expended cumulatively, with no breakdown of the figures. It must be borne in mind that the payments covered land purchase, fees and overheads as well as instalments under the contract.

Year	receipts £	payments £	balance £
1819	30,105-0-0	27,465-8-10	2,639-11-2
1820	71,995-0-0	70,634-11-2	1,310-8-11
1821	107,042-9-8	108,591-11-2	-1,549-1-6
1822	140,954-2-0	140,016-19-1	937-2-11
1823	162,709-10-3	158,438-1-7	4271-8-8

Some of the receipts came from two Exchequer loans of £24,000 and £16,000 which were repayable at 4% interest[23] whilst most of the remainder came from share subscriptions. What these figures shew is that, apart from in 1821, there was no shortage of funds available to the Committee during the construction phase.

In the 1819 report the Company stated that *contractors have been regularly paid every month for the works that have been executed, agreeably to the Certificates* of the Company's Resident Engineer...* This gives the impression that all is going swimmingly with the contract. Interestingly, it is the only year that contractual payments are mentioned in the annual report thereby keeping the proprietors in the dark about the gathering storm!

The Big Claim

In the Arundel Castle archive is a 30-page document[24] referencing a contractual claim for additional payments for the works. It was put together by a solicitor acting for Dyson and Thornton, so it naturally gives a rather one-sided view, but we can infer the client's stance from the annual reports and, with the benefit of 180 years of hindsight, we can gain clear insight into the problem – insight which shews neither the Company nor their Resident Engineer, James Hollinsworth, in a very good light.

The document begins by citing the original contract (which is useful since no copy of this document survives) and from this we find that of the fixed-price contract total the sums for the works in the Sussex line were as follows:

	£
Main line Ford to Birdham	40,520
Chichester branch (excl basin)	4,170
Total	44,690

Dyson and Thornton were making a claim for extra payments totalling £32,792-9s-2d† over the original total contract sum of £64,050 equating to an extra 51% - a claim of not-inconsiderable magnitude. As we are being parochial, we will only examine the

* The Resident Engineer would value the work done each month and issue a *certificate* declaring how much the contractor was entitled to be paid by the client.

† This is the sum after some deductions had been made for deleted work

portion of the claim relating to the canals in Sussex which came to £19,003-4s-5d, however many of the principles also applied to the works beyond Birdham. The Sussex part of the claim can be broken down as follows:

	£ s d
• Widening and deepening Birdham-Chichester	6071-12-0
• Building Chichester Basin and Canal Road	6211 –3-11
• Boating 34,000 yd³ spoil to Bersted Valley	850 -0-0
• "Sundry extra works"	5324-10-10
• Repairing riotous damage	545-17-8

The list gives an impression of the scale of the extra work in financial terms, and it is interesting to note that in the case of the £545-17s-8d claimed for the "riotous damage" (see page 26), £346-3s-6d was for legal fees amounting to twice the actual cost of the repairs–'twas ever thus! The "sundry extra works" sum was not broken down, but within the text we find that one item was Hollinsworth's requirement for the aqueduct over the Aldingbourne Rife to be changed from the contacted single opening of 16 feet to two openings of eight feet.

The contractor contends that, notwithstanding the contractual stipulation that the contractor should not carry out any varied work until a price had been agreed, Hollinsworth had instructed verbal variations which had not been backed up by agreements and/or prices and then, as a result, refused to pay for the completed works!

Another complaint was that Hollinsworth had withheld payments on the grounds that ... *some parts of the Works of the Canal have not been properly performed by the contractors.* Now this sort of thing is right and proper since the contract required workmanship and materials to be to the satisfaction of the Engineer and, as we have seen in the case of the arches, the standard of the brickwork was very low. However, the contractor alleged that Hollinsworth had *not, down to the present time, given any requisition...to alter vary or re-execute any part of such works...* and that, therefore, it was fair to presume that the works had all been executed satisfactorily. This would have been a difficult case for the Company to answer, as would the further grouse that Hollinsworth had been withholding more money under retention* than the contract allowed for.

The matter of boating the spoil from Chichester to form the high embankment in the Bersted Valley is most interesting. We learn that the contract precluded any back-cutting (i.e making borrow pits adjacent to the works) except at Bersted, but it allowed the contractor to make *occasional spoil banks.* It seems that, despite these contract provisions, the Company had ordered the spoil to be boated to Bersted in order to save acquiring five acres of land there for a borrow pit, and spreading any surplus material on three-and-a-half acres of land at Chichester.

Although the £850 extra-cost of this had been agreed, the effects upon the programme had not been taken into account. Building on this fact, the final plank in the claim was that, despite the considerably-increased scope, the Company still expected the contractor to complete the navigation in the time he had contracted for the original works, and that they would not waive the £10,000 penalty for late completion. The contractors calculated that, based upon 50 boats each carrying 12 cubic yards during a five-day week, the changed method of working would take an extra 56 weeks and 3 days!

There are many colourful conclusions drawn about the actions of the Company and its Resident Engineer, one of which is the solicitor's opinion that their actions resulted from *...a more base, unprincipled and shameful attempt to cheat and defraud than made by any individual body of men.* Strong stuff indeed!

Letters cited in the claim make it clear that by August 1823 Dyson and Thornton had withdrawn their labour and relinquished all responsibility for the care of the works, and would only return to complete the same when they got paid. The Company's clerk wrote to them pointing out that the Company had referred the matter back to Hollinsworth who had decided the dispute would be decided by

* It is normal practice under a construction contract for the client to retain a percentage of the due sums pending satisfactory completion of the works. In this case the retention sum was 10% but was only to be applied to the first half of the contract sum.

Mr Telford. In other words they were going to arbitration, and the arbitrator was to be the great Thomas Telford (1757-1834) a civil engineer superior in status even to John Rennie and who, in 1820, became the first president of the Institution of Civil Engineers. It would not have been possible to find a more eminent arbitrator and that they were prepared to lay such a case before Telford suggests that Dyson and Thornton felt very sure of their facts.

Looking at it from this distance it can be seen that if the Company had made a concerted effort to cheat the contractors out of their due payments it was not on account of having insufficient funds available so had they already begun to have fears about the project's viability? Was Hollinsworth simply acting unprofessionally in being so inequitable in his obligations under the contract, or had the Company been steering his judgements in this direction? We will never know for there is no record of the outcome of the arbitration, or even whether it got that far, but it is interesting to surmise what the Great Man might have ruled had it done so. He certainly would have criticised the Contractor's poor workmanship, and Hollinsworth's non-rejection of it, and might have been horrified at Hollinsworth's seemingly unprofessional approach. He would doubtless also have condemned the naïve and penny-pinching approach that the Company had adopted towards the contract.

Interestingly in the report of their special general meeting held on 21 December 1824[25] the Committee of Management refer to the sum they had allowed in the accounts for damages and completing the canal (£10,000) thinking that it may be *rather overrated ...as the amount of the latter must in great measure depend upon the result of the Arbitration now depending between the Company and the Contractors.* Until copies of reports after 1824 come to light the outcome must remain a mystery.

The claim does however suggest a possible explanation for the use of swing bridges in the occupation works between Ford and Hunston Junction; on the face of it a curious provision since cast-iron opening structures would, at that time, generally have been more expensive than arches made from bricks produced on site. All the swing-bridge sites occur where the canal bed is at, or just below, existing ground level, so the relative levels would have required a higher arch structure than one spanning a cutting or sidelong ground. Higher arches require longer and wider approach earthworks which could thus be pushed outside the limits of deviation* in which case the Company would not have had the necessary powers of compulsory purchase. This last would not have been a problem on highway bridges where the road was owned by the parish council who stood to be relieved of their responsibility for maintenance. What Dyson and Thornton's claim demonstrates is that the Company were so keen to avoid creating borrow pits in the Bersted Valley, owing to the high cost of buying land outside the limits of deviation, that they preferred to boat spoil in to form the earthworks. So, as swing bridges required very little in the way of approach slopes, it could be on balance that for "level" locations, by obviating the need for importing extra fill and purchasing expensive land outside the limits of deviation, they became the cheaper option.

In business

At length, despite the contractual wranglings, the navigation was ready for business and an early opinion about its usefulness is given in *Priestley's Navigable Rivers and Canals* of 1831[26]:

> *This is a stupendous work, and from its connexion with others, as seen by the inspection of our map, opens a communication with about every part of our Kingdom; its utility, therefore, is self-evident. By the execution of it, military stores may also be transmitted inland from London to Portsmouth, which would avoid the risks that transport would otherwise incur in time of war, by the necessity of going through the Straits of Dover and coastwise.*

Unfortunately few traders had headed this glowing recommendation.

---

* Limits of deviation set the boundaries for the land which can be compulsorily purchased to build the works.

References Chapter III

---

[1] WRSO Raper M297
[2] Green, Alan H J St John's Chapel and the New Town Phillimore 2005
[3] WRSO Raper M298 Report of Committee of Management, August 1818
[4] Hadfield, Charles The Canals of South and South East England
[5] WRSO Raper M299 to 303
[6] WSRO QDP/W34 Rennie's deposited plan for the 1817 Bill indicates this level on the long section
[7] WSRO Raper M300 Report of Committee of management May 1820
[8] Heneghan , FD The Chichester Canal, CP11 Chichester City Council 1958
[9] Institution of Civil Engineers REN/RB/10/318
[10] Verbal evidence of Mr Casher-Soffe, a descendent of Edward Casher.
[11] WSRO QDP/W34
[12] WSRO Raper M300 op cit
[13] WRSO Raper M299
[14] Arundel Castle ArchiveMD 2525, Statement of Reference in case between the Canal Company and Dyson and Thornton, includes the cost of repairs.
[15] WSRO C/3 Common Council Minute Book 1783-1826
[16] The City of Chichester Guide, 16th edition 1957, Chichester City Council. Plate 4 is an engraving of the antiquary Thomas King which illustrates some of the coins.
[17] Heneghan FD, CP11 op cit
[18] WSRO MF1170 John Marsh Journals 1819-1823
[19] WSRO MF 1170 op cit
[20] Vine PAL London's Lost Route to the Sea, David & Charles 1986
[21] Heneghan FD, CP 11 op cit
[22] ibid
[23] WSRO Raper M304 statement to proprietors for Special General Meeting 21 December 1824
[24] Arundel Castle MD 2525 op cit
[25] WSRO Raper M304 op cit
[26] pp 527-531. *Priestley* was reprinted by David & Charles in 1969.

CHAPTER IV

Unfulfilled ambitions 1823-1891

The new route to Portsmouth

The 1817 Act set out the commercial rules for running the Portsmouth and Arundel Navigation, including the maximum tolls that could be charged. The 1819 Act allowed the tolls to be increased in order to fund the additional works, and these higher rates applied from the opening, namely:

- Dung, ashes, chalk, marl used as manure 3d/ton mile
- Chalk, marl, limestone etc not as manure 6d/ton mile
- All goods not related to the above 6d/ton mile
- Passage of empty boats at locks 1/6d per lock
- Passengers 2d/mile
- Parcels and packages not exceeding 2 cwt 1½d/mile

An additional form of income was obtainable from the penalties that could be levied against miscreants: the various types of crime and their penalties being listed in Sections CXXVIII to CXXIII of the 1817 Act including:-

- Leaving swing bridges open to the canal £5
- Floating timber or dumping rubbish £5
- Dumping rubbish on towpaths £2
- Wasting water at locks £5
- Destroying banks or buildings up to 14 years Transportation
- Using pointed barge poles £10
- Obstructing the canal £1, then 5/- per hour

The penalties had to be recovered by a Justice of the Peace and, save for the fines for leaving bridges open which were to be shared between the informer and the poor of the parish concerned, the monies were passed to the company after legal expenses ... *to be applied and disposed of towards defraying the expenses of said*

Navigation. Regrettably, we have no records of how much income the Company managed to derive from penalties, or how many vandals were rewarded with a free trip to the Antipodes.

Despite all this statuary guidance the business of the Portsmouth and Arundel Navigation did not get off to an auspicious start, what with the delays to the opening of the Ford to Hunston section and Dyson and Thornton's massive claim. Unfortunately these events were to prove omens for the success of the venture for little, if anything, ever seemed to go in the Company's favour.

In 1824 the 116-mile journey from Portsmouth to London, over the combined routes of the Portsmouth and Arundel, the Arun and the Wey and Arun Navigations, normally took four days[1] but only 3,650 tons of cargo were conveyed[2] instead of the predicted 55,000; the reason for the low take up apparently being the problem of securing an adequate cargo to make the return journey profitable. One cargo regularly carried was bullion from Portsmouth to the Bank of England which, in 1830, was passing at the rate of 40 tons per week[3]. These bullion barges were accompanied by armed Redcoats to see off any would-be robbers hoping to stage what would have been a Georgian equivalent of the Great Train Robbery.

The types of vessel using the Navigation varied. Through traffic to London had to be on horse-drawn barges owing to fixed bridges and the tunnel on the Wey and Arun, but between Birdham and Chichester ocean-going sailing barges plied, either under sail or towed by horse according to the state of the wind. The maximum size of vessels permitted over this section at the start was 85 feet length, 18 feet beam and 7 feet draught[4]. The Canal Company owned a steam tug, named *Egremont* in honour of their chief investor, but as she was too wide to use the canal she was employed in towing barges through the harbours between Portsmouth and Birdham. We do not have much in the way of detail about the vessel but we can assume that she was a paddler, and was one of a series of four such steamers[5] who bore the noble name. Section CIX of the 1817 Act was most specific about the types of steam vessel that could be used on the Navigation ... *it shall not be lawful for any person, or persons, to use or employ upon the said channels or harbours, in any boat or vessel, any steam engine in which the steam is blown out into the atmosphere, instead of being condensed by cold water or in which the steam used to work the engine is of a strength equal to double the pressure of the atmosphere.* One can detect a certain nervousness here, but this should not be surprising for in 1817 steam-powered shipping was still in its infancy.

In 1824 alarm bells had begun to ring about the Company's financial position. Not only had the early trading figures been disappointing, the Exchequer loan needed to be repaid and there were still serious problems with the infrastructure. A special general meeting was called on 21 December 1824 to lay before shareholders the sorry facts that the Company had a debt of £49,864, and the annual cost of running the business - £4,424 - was not being matched by the income £1,650[6]. It was resolved at the meeting to raise £20,000 by a voluntary call of £10 per shareholder and to put a Bill before the next Parliamentary session to obtain the necessary powers. In the wordy report to the meeting, the Company stated that such a call was necessary to *save the canal from that ruin which otherwise awaits it.* They then tried to put an optimistic gloss on the chances of interest being paid on the requested investment by saying that *...the Committee have great satisfaction in stating that under all the adverse circumstances with which they have had to contend from the incomplete and defective condition in which the Contractors have left the Canal, and notwithstanding the prejudice and opposition which has existed, and still exists against it, the Tolls have greatly increased within the last year.* They went on to lament the poor take-up of its facilities but expected that once the canal was finally made adequate and its merits better known .. *the whole if not the greater part of the Trade of the Western Ports and that of Jersey and Guernsey with the Metropolis will be carried on through the medium of the Canal.* Pious hopes indeed – it was to be downhill for most of the way now.

The Bill was defeated by petitioners, but on 18 September 1826 the Company's chief supporter, Lord Egremont, announced in the *Hampshire Telegraph* that he had voluntarily surrendered his holding of 315 shares (valued at £15,750 on issue) and had offered to repay the Exchequer Loans of £40,000 for which he had – rashly as it turned out – acted as guarantor. This represented an unbelievably magnanimous gesture on his behalf, especially as he had waived his right to any claim for future reimbursement. The only condition he placed on his offer was that *the Proprietors…shall cause the Canal to be rendered complete and efficient, as originally contemplated.*

There is a bitter irony here; so proud had Lord Egremont been with his new investment that he commissioned JMW Turner to paint it in oils. This painting, of which two versions were produced, is probably the most famous painting of Chichester and was made from a point near Poyntz Bridge at Hunston, with the cathedral in the background.

The Rennie Report – and its aftermath

The problems encountered with the state of the infrastructure had caused the Company and The Lord High Admiral to seek the advice of John Rennie Junior (Later *Sir John*) who, with his brother, carried out an inspection of the whole navigation and delivered a 14-page report[7] on 4 October 1827. The Admiralty had became involved because, as the report states, Lord Egremont had suggested that the Government might wish to become the principal shareholder in the canal. John Rennie found the Sussex main line to be *…still in a very imperfect state; for a considerable portion of its length it has not been puddled at all and the remainder is insufficiently puddled… it is consequently incapable of holding water…*again reflecting badly upon the Contractors and Resident Engineer. He also found that all bridges were in need of brickwork repairs, the decks of the swing-bridges required replacing, the towpaths needed gravelling and the fences were practically non-existent. On the Chichester branch *puddle gutters*[*] were required to but cut along the west and south sides of the basin and all the way along the west bank of the canal to the junction together with repairs to Poyntz and Padwick bridges. John Rennie compiled detailed estimates for the works (including the £6,159 option of creating a new cut at Portsbridge across the top of Portsea Island) and provided an analysis of the company's fortunes.

---

[*] Puddle gutters were deep slit trenches sunk alongside leaking water courses and filled with puddle clay. Today this is known as diaphragm walling.

The total expenditure needed to put the Sussex line *into complete repair* was estimated at £20,083-12-11 which, when added to the costs of dredging across the harbours, putting the Portsea line into a similar state of repair[†] and paying off outstanding debts, required the sum of £49,227 to be raised. John Rennie Junior also pointed out that in 1827 the cost of constructing the Portsmouth and Arundel Navigation stood at £176,314 – 42% higher than his father's estimate. The one thing we are not told is the magnitude of the Rennies' fee!

Spurred on by this, the Company prepared another Bill to go before Parliament to enable them to raise money by share issue. It was enacted on 23 May 1828[*] entitled *An Act for granting further Powers for the Company of Proprietors of the Portsmouth and Arundel Navigation.* The Act, in 32 sections, recites the earlier legislation and refers to the debts with which the Company had been *burthened* and in its preamble presents to His Majesty the sorry saga about how ... *the said undertaking is in an unfinished State and many parts thereof have, from Disuse and Want of the necessary Funds for keeping the same in repair, fallen into Decay; from all of which several Circumstances the said Undertaking will soon be in danger of becoming useless, unless the same be speedily and effectively completed and repaired.* The Act empowered the Company to raise up to £50,000 by the issue of £25 shares; such shares having preference over previous issues and paying 6% for the first ten years and 5% thereafter. There was an if-all-else-fails provision enabling sum to be raised by a mortgage if the call for shares was not answered. This time the tolls were not amended.

The share issue duly went ahead and hapless investors poured more money into a moribund venture from which they were destined never to receive any dividend.

The second share issue was not the only means of raising money explored by the Company, for they also looked to sell off their surplus land. Under Section VIII of the 1817 Act, where the canal bisected a parcel of land and the residual portions were less than one

---

[†] It was empty and disused when the Rennies saw it in 1827.

[*] 9 Geo IV Cap lvii

Portsmouth and Arundel
NAVIGATION COMPANY

New SHARE No. 720

This is to Certify that Baden Powell of [illegible] Kent Esquire

is proprietor of ONE SHARE in the PORTSMOUTH and ARUNDEL NAVIGATION numbered as above and Registered in the Register Book of the Company Subject to the Rules, Orders and Regulations of the said Company, and that he, his Executors, Administrators and Assigns are intitled to the Profits and Advantages thereof.

Dated this [illegible] day of March 18[illegible]

[illegible]
PORTSMOUTH
Clerk to the Company.

Fig 7. A share certificate in the Portsmouth and Arundel Navigation from the second issue in 1829, entitling the holder to the profits and advantages thereof. What it lacked in investment value it tried to make up for in its appearance! (Roger Dunbar collection) acre, the promoters were obliged to purchase the whole parcel from the landowner. One place where this had happened was Hunston in respect of parcels 6,7 and 8 shewn on the Deposited Plans. In 1829 the Company offered to re-sell the severed lands to the original owners, Major General Crosbie, Charles Smith and the Dean and Chapter respectively, but the gist of their response was *no*; the Clerk to the Company swearing affidavits on 23 October 1829[8] to the effect that the offer had been...*wholly refused by them.* Not to be deterred the Company attempted to sell the lands. to Samuel Tufnell but another affidavit confirmed that he too had declined their kind offer. Finally they decided to sell all the Hunston lands, and also a surplus plot adjacent to Canal Road, by auction. The sale took place on 4 April 1829 at the Richmond Arms Inn at the head of the basin under the gavel of Mr King[9] and the Hunston lands were knocked down to George Dibden for £60/acre.

The Richmond Arms* was situated at the west end of the Chichester basin and, along with the similar Egremont Arms adjacent to Saltern's lock, opened at the same time as the canal offering the bargees rest and refreshment. Built of flint below a slate roof it blended in well with the other new buildings around the basin but refreshment and auction sales were not the only things it had to offer for on 2 July 1828 there took place a public sparing match between *Ned Neal and Whiteheaded Bob, assisted by Isle of Wight HALL and several amateurs.* The poster[10] stated that the two protagonists *Being recovered from their late Fight intend giving their Friends at Chichester a rare treat of the ART OF SELF DEFENCE.* The event was advertised to take place in the *Large Room* of the Inn, and there were to be two performances, at two in the afternoon and seven in the evening. Admission was a staggering 2/6d for each session so the audience would have had to have been very keen on the art of self defence to attend!

The revenue figures for the first five years[11] which were unearthed by the Rennies during their investigation did not provide encouraging reading:

---

* It was recently renamed *the Waterside* losing its historic link.

Year	Revenue (£)
1822 (May-Dec)	142-7-8
1823	669-9-11
1824	826-12-5
1825	994- 6-6
1826	1,010- 3-9
1827 (Jan-Jul)	533-17-6

The figure for 1822 is low because in addition to its being for only a half year, the main line between Hunston and Ford had still not opened. The 1826 revenue was derived from the carriage of 13,351 tons of goods and the split[12] of the £1,010 is interesting:

Section	Revenue (£)
Birdham-Chichester	428-6-8
Birdham-Ford	17-3-3
Ford or Chichester to Birdham	564-3-10

The dubious viability of the Hunston to Ford section is only too obvious, but there does seem to have been an increase in traffic following a lowering of tolls in March 1830 when it was recorded that trade between London and Portsmouth was *becoming very brisk* with regular and well-loaded barges plying. Cargoes included 84 tons of marble from the Mediterranean and another 20 tons from Asia for the King at Windsor all within the space of a week[13].

The dearth of annual reports after 1824 is frustrating, but one for 1831 has survived[14] which gives the outcome of the Rennies' recommendations and shews that the Committee of Management were still putting a brave face on things. The 1831 Annual General Meeting had been postponed from the 17 May to 7 June, *to ensure a more full attendance,* and in the written report they state that the all the Works have now been satisfactorily completed, with the repairs on the Sussex Line of the Canal proving substantial and that a warehouse and an additional crane had been provided at the Chichester Basin. There is also an intriguing entry regarding water supply on the Sussex canals:

...it is confidently expected that the Steam Engine which was retained for occasional supply of water in case of need, will not henceforth be required, as the present natural supplies will prove sufficient...the Company not having yet had occasion to resort to the water from a mill which they purchased in order to command a sufficiency in the driest seasons.

In their 1827 report, the Rennies had opined that it would be desirable to obviate the steam pump at Ford by finding some natural source, and this the Company had obviously tried to do, but the identity of the mill, and the reason why it was necessary to buy it, is not stated. A likely candidate was Runcton Mill, situated on the Pagham Rife and not far from the canal. This mill was downstream from where the Pagham Rife passed beneath the canal and so, if the waters of the rife had been harnessed to provide a feed, the mill's lifeblood would have been cut off thus creating a need to acquire it and close it down.

The Company goes on to report that in Portsmouth the new Portsbridge cut was open and the now-abandoned Portsea canal was being filled in and offered for sale. On a gloomier note they regretted that they had not raised more money by share issue as at that time *the purchase of the Mill and Stream was not then contemplated.* This suggests that the property had not been acquired cheaply and, in view of the fact it had not proved necessary, that the Company had made another blunder. They mention that the coal trade into Chichester had been diminished by the effects of a colliers' strike in the north and a proposed reduction in duty, but felt that it would recover. It should be pointed out here that much of the imported coal was going to the gasworks which had opened in 1823 just north of the basin. The final short paragraph of the report is worth quoting in full:

The trade from London to Chichester has been on the advance, and while your Committee lament that they cannot yet report a trade to Portsmouth, they have the satisfaction of stating that the trade to Chichester alone, after paying all the charges for management and current repairs, realises a small surplus.

It was necessary to turn the page to the accounts to learn how small the *small surplus* was - £38-16-11! The brief accounts shew that income from tolls amounted to £1028-7-2 and land sales had brought in £546. It also shews that sums of £229-3-0 and £142-9-2 had been expended on works to the Sussex line. The Chairman who prepared the report was Edward Casher, after whom the lock at Birdham was named, but in the election at this meeting he was replaced by W C Newland.

Fig 8. An etching of Padwick Bridge by IJ Wilson C1890 shewing the bridge open to the canal. Note the fender stones to ensure that approaching carts were correctly aligned (WSRO)

We saw in Chapter III how the Chichester builder William Brooks was admonished by the Company for submitting his tender too late, but he was in receipt of another sternly-worded letter on 24 July 1826. Brooks had been spreading builders' rubble on the Company's road with the intention of having it ground down by cartwheels for use as an ingredient of Roman cement* and in the letter, Messrs Edgecombe, the Company's solicitors, reminded him that he had no right to be doing what he had been doing and informed him that he (Edgecombe) was ...*instructed to commence an action against you if you in any manner interfere with the road or otherwise use it except for the passage to and from your land, and that in a proper manner*

Threats of competition

One potential threat to the Portsmouth and Arundel Navigation and its allied navigations was the series of over-optimistic proposals, made between 1825 and 1828, for a "Grand Ship Canal" between London and Portsmouth via Chichester, adopting a more direct route than that offered by the existing systems. Three separate proposals were put forward, one by the Rennie brothers, one by James Elmes, and one by the outspoken Nicholas Cundy. For Elmes this would have been a return to Chichester since he had carried out a body of work in the City between 1811 and 1814[15]. Cundy's report was published in 1825, but in 1827 he published a pamphlet[16] in which he spent as much time rubbishing Elmes' scheme as he did extolling the virtues of his own! In the event the three existing Navigation Companies had nothing to fear on this score, for these grand proposals came to nought; the real threat was posed by an altogether different from of transportation – the railways – a threat which also meant that any proposal for a Grand Ship Canal would not get beyond report stage.

The Company's fortunes took a fatal dive as a result of railway competition when the London Brighton and South Coast Railway extended their West Coast Line from Shoreham to Chichester in June 1846, with a terminus not far from the basin. In March the following year the railway was extended on westwards, opening to Havant on 15 March and to Portsmouth the following June. The effect on the canal was rapid since the railway offered much faster journey times

---

* Roman, or Parker's, Cement is a mixture of lime and siliceous material which produces an immensely strong and waterproof render. Bricks and tiles crushed on a road provided a cheap source for the siliceous material.

for goods between London and Portsmouth, and by 1853 the Ford to Hunston section, already little used since through traffic to London ceased in September 1838,[17] was closed. Meetings of the Committee of Management also became infrequent and in 1849 one shareholder, Sir Charles Burrell, inscribed this lament on his portfolio[18] *These I subscribed for at the desire of Lord Selsey – but which by mismanagement of the canal across the Freshes of the sea have not paid out any interest & probably never will.*

The railways spread quickly in Sussex, the network including lines up the Arun Valley to Horsham and Guildford and along the Rother Valley to Petworth and Midhurst. The three navigation companies tried desperately to compete by lowering their tolls but to no avail – the proverbial writing was on the wall.

There had been several proposals to build a railway to Bognor and the successful one, by the Bognor Railway Company, was authorised by an Act of 1861*. This was to be a single-track branch leaving the West Coast line of the LB&SCR at Barnham and running in a south westerly direction to the resort. Naturally, this railway needed to cross the now-closed main line of the Portsmouth and Arundel which it did approximately one mile from Barnham, at a point where the canal bed was at ground level retained by embanking. The deposited plans[19] for the railway indicated that its line would also be more or less at ground level slicing right through the canal's bunds four feet below the tow-path. The Canal Company had obviously petitioned the Railway Bill in an attempt to protect their interests which resulted in the curious Section 38 of the Act:-

> *The* [railway]*Company shall, in the event of the said Navigation being required for use by Water Traffic, or if the same shall be converted into a Road or Railway, raise the level of the Railway five feet above the levels shewn on the deposited section and shall carry the same by a swing bridge across the said Navigation, Road or Railway and further shall open the said Swing Bridge at all times for the passage of traffic lawfully conveyed on such Navigation, Road or Railway,*

---

* 24&25 Vict Cap 120

But that was not all – Section 40 imposed a £10 fine on the railway company for each occasion that the swing bridge being open to rail traffic delayed traffic on the waterway!

It was intended that the Bognor Railway would be taken over by the LB&SCR from its opening in 1864[20] so they would have taken a keen interest in the passage of the Bill, and the Canal Company's petitioning thereof. Having looked at the canal - now an empty and overgrown ditch - and knowing all about the precarious standing of the Canal Company, the LB&SCR took the risk of agreeing to the draconian provisions in the Bill secure in the knowledge that the chances of having to raise the level of their railway and provide a swing bridge were very small. Some sources have suggested that instead of a swing bridge a fixed bridge was provided here but there is no drawing of such a structure at Network Rail's Plan Arch at Waterloo and the 1:2500-scale Ordnance Survey map of 1875 clearly shews the canal and railway intersecting at the same level. There *was* no structure; to have provided one would have been utterly pointless as its soffit would have been below canal bed level! The LB&SCR's gamble paid off since the need for the swing bridge was never to arise.

Railway competition forced the closure of the Wey and Arun Navigation in July 1871[21] but in 1868, just before it did, one JB Dashwood, accompanied by his wife and a dog improbably named Buz, made a journey along it from Weybridge, destined for Portsmouth. The story of his journey, in a pleasure boat named Caprice, he published as *The Thames to Solent by Canal and Sea*[*] and if this sounds to you rather like Jerome K Jerome's *Three men in a boat* you would be right. The difference is that this was a true tale, whereas Jerome's classic book was fiction – and written 21 years later.

When the intrepid adventurers reached Bramley they made an unhappy discovery:

Our little vessel being so small, we had not intended to proceed to sea in her until we reached Chichester harbour, for on examining

[*] Fortunately this delightful book has been re-published by Shepperton Swan and dedicated to the Wey and Arun Canal Trust from whom it can be obtained.

the maps we found a canal marked out between Ford, near Arundel, to Chichester harbour; this we had meant to use, and sailing from Chichester harbour to come out into the Solent at Langstone Harbour and Hayling Island. Mr Stanton[the lock keeper] *informed us to our dismay that this canal no longer exists; in fact there is now but small trace of it. He said it had not been used for eleven years*[†], *had been trodden in by cattle, filled- in in places and was now quite dry.*

Such a pity! Had it been open we would have had not only a delightful description of the route of the Sussex line but a first-hand account of the operation of those swing bridges. The helpful lock keeper was obviously unaware that a railway had now been added to the list of obstructions.

The end of the Navigation Company

With the closure of both the Portsea canal and the Sussex line east of Hunston Junction, less than half of the waterway remained, but the section between Birdham and Chichester continued to generate a meagre trade into the city. This was insufficient for the Company to justify maintaining staff at Chichester so the tolls were collected on their behalf by Stephen Purchase, a tenant coal merchant who traded at the basin[22]. Other businesses being conducted at Chichester basin at this time, as listed in the various trade directories, included those of George Tyler, beer retailer, John Cover, timber merchant[*], Clement Sayers, lime burner (whose address was given as the Richmond Arms) plus James Sayers, James Biffen and William Rusper coal merchants whose yards were situated on the north side of the basin next to the gasworks wall. Boat building seems to have continued, for in 1861 the boys of Oliver Whitby School[23] were taken to the basin witness the launch of a new Selsey lifeboat.

The Corporation made use of the canal basin for drainage purposes, apparently without the consent of the Canal Company, for

---

† This, if true, would put the closure date at 1857.

* Covers are still in business today. They lived in the house in their yard to the south of the basin, which is now occupied by Geoffrey Osborne Ltd.

they laid an 18 inch culvert† in the Company's road from Market Road to the basin to serve as an overflow conduit for the River Lavant culvert[24]. They connected another drain into this from the police station grounds in 1888 and later a further drain was laid from the railway yards across Stockbridge Road into the north-west corner of the basin[25]. The question of the ownership of Canal Road was raised by Cllr Edney on 20 January 1888[26] but no reply was ever given so the Corporation obviously assumed some sort of divine right over it!

As we have seen no dividends were ever paid and the incompetence of the company was aggravating shareholders, a group of whom, led by James William Ozzard, decided in June 1888 to petition for the winding up of the Company. News of this reached the Corporation who were somewhat alarmed about the pending closure of the City's canal and, at their meeting of 20 July 1888, they resolved[27] both to oppose the petition and to follow counsel's advice that they try to enter into an agreement with the Company before going to court. The solicitor was instructed to draw up heads of agreement regarding the promotion of a Parliamentary Bill which would vest the Birdham to Chichester part of the Navigation in the Corporation ... *the costs of the Bill and putting that part of the canal which is vested in the Corporation into repair be paid out of monies in hand. Any surplus and proceeds of sale of superfluous lands to be assets of shareholders.* The winding-up order was made by Mr Justice North on 4 August 1888 and William Edmonds was awarded the thankless task of being the liquidator[28]. The Corporation met with the liquidator and carried out a survey[29] of the wharfs and buildings at Chichester, estimating that the income from rentals would net £80 per annum. Things then seem to have moved rather slowly for it was not until the Council meeting of 18 December 1891[30] that the Corporation and the liquidator agreed and sealed the lengthy wording of the petition to go into the Bill. In it they cite the shareholders' petition for winding up the Portsmouth and Arundel Company and also the agreement made regarding the vesting. They

† It is still there; in the 1994 floods your author watched with alarm as the head of water in the culvert was sufficient to cause a small fountain to issue forth from the manhole in Basin Road.

also say that *for thirty years and upwards prior to the presentation of the winding-up petition...no meeting of the Company nor of the Committee of Management...was held and the greater part of the said canal has been dried up and disused.* It was signed and sealed by A S Bostock the Mayor, Edward Arnold the Town Clerk and William Edmonds the liquidator, and duly sent off to the parliamentary agents who were drafting the Bill.

The remains of Portsmouth and Arundel Navigation were poised to go into public ownership.

References Chapter IV

[1] Vine PAL, London's lost route to the Sea, David & Charles 1986
[2] ibid
[3] Gates, William G *Illustrated history of Portsmouth* 1900
[4] Heneghan FD *The Chichester Canal* CP11 Chichester City Council 1958
[5] ibid
[6] WSRO Raper M304 Report of the Committee of Management to the meeting
[7] Instituition of Civil Engineers REN/RB/4/93-107
[8] WSRO Add MS 1960 Abstract of Title of the Company to the lands in Hunston.
[9] WSRO Add MS 1959 Sale particulars for the auction.
[10] Andrew Berriman, private collection
[11] REN/RB/4/93-107 op cit which cites the revenues.
[12] ibid
[13] Gates, William G, Illustrated History of Portsmouth, 1900
[14] Portsmouth City Library LP626
[15] Green Alan HJ, St John's Chapel and the New Town Chichester, Phillimore 2005
[16] Institution of Civil Engineers archive 1827 CUNRGS
[17]Vine PAL op cit
[18] WSRO Burrell MSS XXI/H/1
[19] WSRO QDP/W132
[20] Jordan, S, The Bognor branch line, Oakwood Press 1989
[21] Vine PAL op cit
[22] Heneghan F.D, CP11 op cit
[23] Hughes, Peter J, Oliver Whitby School, Chichester, - a history, Phillimore 2002
[24] WSRO C/17 Chichester Common Council Minute Book 1881-1892
[25] ibid
[26] WSRO C/16 Chichester Common Council Minute Book 1885-1888
[27] ibid
[28] Cited in preamble to the Chichester Canal Transfer Act 1892
[29] WSRO Add MS 14399
[30] WSRO C/17 op cit

CHAPTER V

A lingering death 1892-1956

Fig 9 A barge, The Fanny, on the Chichester branch, just north of Hunston Junction, circa 1900. It is a coastal vessel and is proceeding under full sail. It can be seen that there are two smartly-dressed female passengers on board.

(Andrew Berriman collection)

A new beginning?

The Bill transferring ownership to Chichester Corporation was enacted on 27 June 1892 becoming the *Chichester Canal Transfer Act 1892**.

* 55 & 56 Vict. Cap cxxxviii

Following a heavy three-page preamble, which included the Corporation's petition, the Act's 22 sections empowered, inter alia :

- The Chichester portion of the canal to be vested in Chichester Corporation
- The Company and shareholders to be released from their obligations in respect of this part of the canal
- The Corporation to assume the responsibilities of the former Committee of Management
- The Corporation to improve the waterway and its works as necessary
- The Corporation to borrow further monies to maintain and develop the canals business.

Section 7 provided an escape clause for the Corporation in that, if after 1898 the burden on the borough rate outweighed the advantages of keeping the canal open, they could close it and sell off the land and property, the proceeds being credited to the borough coffers. A schedule to the Act provides a description of the canal and listed the assets to be transferred to the Corporation which included Canal Road and the two cottages at its southern end, the buildings on the wharfs and all the bridges, locks and keepers' cottages along the canal's length.

This was now the fifth Act to be passed relating to the Portsmouth and Arundel Navigation and if there were any hopes that it would herald a new beginning they were soon to be dashed. However, before we look at how the new regime fared, we should examine what happened to the shareholders under the liquidation proceedings.

One of those shareholders was Sir Charles Burrell Bart.of 12 Grosvenor Square London, who received, along with other investors, a printed notice from the liquidator regarding the return of share capital.[1] The news it contained cannot have been very encouraging for the first and final payments, to be made on 26 August 1895, were quoted as follows:

- On £50 shares £2-11s-4½d
- On £25 shares £1-5s-8¼d

Sir Charles was informed that the return of capital on his £200 investment was to be £10-5-6 (a loss of 94.87%) and then, to add insult to injury, the solicitors would be charging a handling fee of 5/- per share - i.e. he was about to lose another 1%!

Fig 10. Site of Hunston Junction C1920 looking towards Birdham The photographer is standing in the bed of the abandoned main line from Ford on the site of the brick arch which carried the road over the canal. (Outram Collection, North Mundham PCC)

The liquidator had to raise the funds to make returns to shareholders by selling off the Company's assets, consisting chiefly of land and buildings both in Portsmouth and on the route between Ford and Hunston, all valued at £182,403. The Duke of Richmond purchased two stretches of the latter in 1890 for £162[2], one at Barnham and one in Oving parish, the latter running west from the Bognor road. Correspondence between the liquidator and the Duke's solicitors[3] records the first of many removals of bridges on the abandoned Sussex line when, in 1891, the former wrote to say that the brick arch carrying the Chichester to Bognor road (now the A259) was to be demolished and the contractor, a Mr Binsted of Runcton, was to use the surplus materials for infilling *in that portion of the canal.* Many other such sales took place as is witnessed by the majority of the canal bed now being in private ownership.

The New Broom

The Corporation put the responsibility for running the canal onto an existing multi-purpose committee[4], which now assumed the title of *The Highways, Paving, Lighting and Canal Committee.* One of its early resolutions was to ban barges from using the canal when it was frozen in the months of December and January, and they erected a notice at Salterns Lock stating that barges must not be used to break up the ice during those months. Presumably it was permissible for a bargee to beak the ice in February! The Committee was obviously concerned about the continually-falling tonnages, which had dropped in 1896 to a mere 704 of sand and grit,[5] but at their meeting on 31 July[6] that year they resolved to keep the canal open *as the indirect advantage ... is greatly in excess of the actual cost.* Someone had suggested that the bed be planted with osiers,[*] a typical Victorian idea which was quashed on the grounds that it would add to the financial burden. Mr Purchase, the tenant coal merchant who acted as toll collector when the Canal Company withdrew their staff from the basin, continued to act in this capacity for the Corporation, but in July 1897 the Committee resolved that it would be cheaper for the Corporation Collector to perform this duty so Mr Purchase's services were dispensed with. Another tenant the Corporation inherited was the Chichester Rowing Club, who operated from a boathouse at the basin. In May 1898 the club owed six-years' rent (30/-) and in response to the Collector's demands[7] the secretary thereof stated that the club was defunct and had no funds with which to pay. However, the boathouse still contained the club's vessels which the Corporation seized, and the wily Mr Purchase then offered to buy for 30/- thus setting their books straight.

[*] i.e.Willow trees

The Selsey Tramway

In 1895 another railway began to affect the canal when the redoubtable Colonel Stephens proposed the construction of the Hundred of Manhood and Selsey Tramway between Chichester and Selsey. It was to be built under the forthcoming 1896 Light Railway Act which dispensed with the need for formal powers and, as it was to be designated a tramway, the provision of niceties such as signalling as well. The Common Council felt that the line would be of great advantage and resolved to assist by selling off any land at a fair valuation and would even allow it to be carried along the eastern side of the canal. However they were concerned about how the railway might cross the canal and be able to cater for masted vessels. In a letter to them,[8] the Colonel described his proposed *drawbridge*[†] and its modus operandi, saying that ...*a man will always be available to work the bridge and a telephone or bell will be provided at the bridge in case communication is required...* An agreement was drafted to cover the canal crossing which specified that *the bridge be placed in the centre of the canal in the same way and to the same width as Donnington bridge.*[9]

The crossing point was just to the west of Hunston (canal) junction, and the structure was a half-bascule bridge formed of rolled wrought-iron joists supported on a mass-concrete abutment on the north bank of the canal[10] It was raised by two independent winches rigged with chains and pulley blocks hung from a portal frame spanning the track. The crossing was made on a high skew, but the structure itself was made square by pushing the abutment into the canal on the north side and providing a short approach embankment from the south, which also gave the minimum opening needed. Hefty timber fender piles provided protection from collisions with barges.

Construction took place in July 1897 and, to facilitate the casting of the abutment, the water level was lowered by building a temporary dam across the canal at Hunston. Unfortunately the dam burst

---

[†] This was a misnomer, what he was proposing was actually a half bascule bridge (as a Civil Engineer he should have known better!) he doubtless used the term as its operation was reminiscent of a drawbridge on a castle

flooding the works and the Colonel had to write to protest to the Corporation pointing out the serious loss to the Tramway company.[11]

The completed bridge was fully in compliance with the eccentric nature of all Colonel Stephen's ventures and had a decidedly economic, not to say flimsy, air about it. Amongst the Colonel's economies was the failure to provide any decking timbers for the convenience of the patrolmen walking across the bridge. Raising the bridge required the two winch-men to wind at exactly the same speed so as to avoid the superstructure wracking and jamming – which it frequently did, being stuck in the up position on one occasion for two days[12].

However the process of opening the bridge for barge traffic was not speedy since, not only had the winch-men to travel to the bridge, they had first to remove fishplates in the track before commencing the lift, and complaints from bargees about the inordinate times they were kept waiting rolled in from the start. The Town Clerk had to write to Colonel Stephens on several occasions telling him to abide by the agreement with respect to the delays, and on one such[13] hinted that the Corporation might take proceedings to ensure that he did.

Fig 11 The bridge carrying the Selsey Tramway over the canal at Hunston c1896. The bridge has been raised to allow a sailing barge to pass through. *(Chichester District Museum)*

Under the agreement ownership of the completed structure was vested in the Corporation who charged the Tramway Company £2 per annum for its use. The Selsey Tramway was to be short lived but it managed to outlast the canal over whose troubled waters it now strode.

Cash ebbs and flows

Faced with dwindling tolls the Committee had to come up with some ideas for making economies. Their highest maintenance liability was the pair of locks at Birdham, particularly the lower one (Salterns), which bore the ravages of the tides. In November 1898 the Committee accepted that new gates were required for Salterns lock and so sought tenders for the supply and installation of the same. The successful tenderer was J D Foster, a shipwright whose yard was at Emsworth, but, as even his price was higher than anticipated, the City Surveyor was ordered to negotiate with Mr Foster to see whether he would re-quote for supplying the gates only, leaving installation to the Corporation. The nature of the exchanges is not recorded but it was not until 24 February 1899 that the Committee instructed the City Surveyor[14] to proceed with erecting one new gate and repairing the other in conjunction with Mr Foster at a cost not exceeding £100. Further repairs were required to the lock gates in the autumn of 1902 and, of the £100 cost, £40 was for building a temporary dam across the canal to allow the water to be drained off.

The Committee also came up with some new initiatives for deriving revenue from the canal. The potential for charging for leisure activities was spotted early on and in September 1904 a fee of 5/- was levied for each pleasure boat using the canal. It was also observed that drivers of traction engines were drawing water from the canal basin and so the Committee decided, in 1910, to grant annual licences for this at 10/-, but also allowing occasional users to water their engines for 6d a time[15]. Unfortunately these charges were frequently flouted; Mr Ansell, the wharfinger, reported that many enginemen were refusing to pay the drawing fee so he was instructed to record names and times of offenders whilst lock keepers were instructed to check the names of pleasure boats against the accounts and to report any new arrivals.

The only regular cargoes coming into the basin by 1906 were barges of coal and shingle[16] and the last recorded working occurred that year, leaving the Corporation bereft of income from tolls. However they did not declare the waterway closed and lived in hopes of better times to come whilst the abstraction of the canal water for cooling purposes, by both the gas and electric light companies who operated near its shores, brought in some additional remuneration. Responsibility for maintaining the canal was transferred to the *Lighting, Fire Brigade and Canal Committee* from 1910.

Amongst the many leased properties surrounding the basin was an ice works which was situated at its east end near the former electricity generating station. Started by the *West Sussex Pure Ice and Cold Storage Co* the lease was transferred in 1923 to L W Barnes who later purchased it outright in 1928.

Fig. 12 Members of the City Club dressed as the gun crew of "HMS Chichester" marking the 1911 Coronation at the canal basin. To the left of the picture can be seen the ice works and opposite, on the south wharf, are some of Cover's un-sawn tree trunks. (Chichester District Museum)

The bridge problem

The advent of horseless carriages and commercial vehicles brought a new problem for the Corporation in respect of the cast-iron swing bridges carrying the public highway across the canal at Donnington and Birdham; Crosbie and Cutfield Bridges respectively. When Rennie designed these* he only had in mind horse-drawn carts for which the structures were eminently suited. However with the increased axle loadings of the twentieth century the bridges soon began to shew signs of distress; the timber decks broke up and the cast iron members, having an intense dislike of being put into tension, fractured.

As early as 1905 complaints had been received from Westhampnett Rural District Council, the highway authority, about the state of the bridges and the Committee resolved on 27 November 1905[17] to replace the superstructure at Donnington with the best of the three bridges not now in use†. It is not known whether this idea was put into practice but the Committee wrote to Westhampnett RDC in June 1906 to advise them that work had been *carried out expeditiously* and hoped that no further repairs would be needed for the foreseeable future. Cutfield bridge at Birdham had also been repaired that year and prohibition notices, restricting the permitted loading, were displayed at both sites which upset the County Council[18] who threatened to deduct £50 from their Secondary Roads Grant if the bridges were not made suitable for ordinary traffic. The following year the Common Council Meeting decided that an approach should be made to Westhampnett RDC to ascertain what contribution they might make to the provision of new bridges; the answer to this was not encouraging.

There then began a 19-year long disagreement between the Corporation and Westhapmpnett RDC about the futures of the bridges. The Corporation, naturally, wished to retain the rights of navigation which could only be preserved by providing new 12- foot

---

* The drawings and specifications for these have not been found so the design cannot be ascribed accurately- it may have been carried out by Hollinsworth on Rennie's behalf.

† These would have been Padwick, Casher and Egremont which were little-used accommodation/occupation bridges

wide swing bridges, whilst Westhampnett, equally naturally, did not wish to pay anymore than they had to, and so opted for a cheaper fixed-bridge solution. The Corporation continued to patch and repair the old bridges rather than replace them, in the face of strong criticism from the ratepayers' associations about the dangers, and it was not until 27 April 1923 that an agreement[19] was entered into between the two parties to replace the swing bridges with culverts. This might at first appear to have been a climb-down by the Corporation - but it was not. In the Agreement, Clause 6 required the Highway Authority (i.e. Westhampnett RDC) to remove the culverts and restore the canal upon the canal operator (the Corporation) giving them 28-days notice thereof. It was a neat solution; the highway authority got a cheap scheme whilst the Corporation protected their option to reopen the canal should the occasion arise

The work was not set to happen too quickly for it was not completed until May 1926[20]. Meanwhile in 1923 Southdown Motor Services were expanding onto the peninsular and in response to the Company's permission to run the services the Corporation stated that they *...expressed the opinion that there is no objection to the Southdown motor buses passing over the bridge at their own risk* (!)

A similar threat from a road-scheme was posed when the Chichester by pass was built just before the Second World War. The by-pass crossed the canal at a point where the latter was in cutting, but mercifully, rather than filling it in, a bridge with navigable headroom was provided. No doubt the implications of another agreement about reinstatement guided this decision.

The Corporation now had to decide what to do with this asset which would continue to be a drain on their resources. The City Surveyor estimated in 1923 that further repairs were needed to the two locks, to the tune of £420 for Casher and £220 for Salterns. This gave the Committee just cause for concern so they instructed the City Surveyor to obtain estimates from J D Foster of Emsworth to dam Casher Lock and repair only Salterns. That really did seem to be the final nail in the coffin but it was not until 9 May 1928 that the Canal Committee decided[21] that it was time to call it a day and close the canal officially under Section 7 of the 1892 Act. Their recommendation was put to the Common Council who approved it on the 6th of June following.

Thereafter the canal entered its wilderness years and photographs taken in the 1930s reveal that the water levels were allowed to drop, leaving only a shallow steam in the centre whereby waters from the various springs that had been harnessed to feed the canal, found their way to the sea. Despite this it provided Mahatma Ghandi with a pleasant early-morning walk[22] one Sunday in October 1931 when he was staying with Bishop Bell.

The lower reach of the canal found a new lease of life when on, 4 May 1932, Mr D S Vernon took a full-repairing lease on the stretch from Cutfield Bridge to Salterns, including both locks and the cottages, for a boat-building venture. In 1934 he assigned the lease to a new organisation, The Chichester Yacht Company, of which he was a director beginning a long and colourful era in the canal's history[23].

Mr Vernon's lease, together with rent from premises at the basin and the canal cottages, now provided the only income from the erstwhile Portsmouth and Arundel Navigation.

The Canal at War

As the clouds of war began to gather in 1939 the City Council formed an emergency committee *to accelerate Civil Defence Plans* which first met on 22 April that year[24], chaired by the Mayor. There were natural fears that Chichester Harbour would provide an ideal spot for the enemy to mount an invasion, and ways were sought to frustrate such knavish tricks. Our canal was rudely wakened from its slumbers to play its part in the war effort when, on 19 August 1942, a "Form of Requisition" was served on the Town Clerk[25] by Admiral Sir William M James KCB in respect of Chichester Yacht Club at Birdham; the clubhouse being required for the billeting of Naval Officers. Then on the 26 August another Form of Requisition was served, this time in respect of the remainder of Mr Vernon's leased property – the shipyard and workshops - together with the canal and locks. The derelict upper lock keeper's cottage had already been requisitioned by the army who demolished it in 1940 in order to salvage the roof timbers.

It was intended to use the canal as an anti-tank defence for which, of course, it needed to be re-filled. What followed could almost have been written as an episode of *Dad's Army* and it spawned a row between the Admiralty, the Corporation and Mr Vernon that was to rumble on long after the war had ended.

Although the Admiralty were in charge of the locks at Birdham, the task of re-filling the canal fell to the Royal Engineers and this part of the story was recently told by Subaltern Hanby-Brown in a Ship Canal Trust newsletter.[26] Subaltern Hanby Brown was put in charge of the operation and advice from an uncle, who was an irrigation inspector in Egypt, was that the canal must be filled as quickly as possible so that the dried-out puddling would swell and seal itself. He discovered the River Lavant overflow culvert, which the Corporation had so thoughtfully provided back in the 1880s,[*] and by damming the river downstream of its junction (the Lavant was in its own culvert beneath Market Avenue at this point) he managed to divert its entire flow into the canal. This produced the desired effect; the canal quickly filled up and held its charge. He then did a deal with a firm who provided and drove a sheet-pile wall across the canal at Birdham, an incentive being that he "gave" them the superstructures of Dudley and Egremont bridges. The rest of the story is to be found in the intriguing correspondence and reports on the Corporation's file.[27]

In January 1943 the City Surveyor's attention was drawn to the fact that the canal was full to overflowing and about to burst its banks in places. Upon investigation he found that the paddles[†] on the lock gates were all locked closed, the keys having been entrusted to a Mr Duff of the boatyard. He sought out Mr Duff and asked that the paddles be opened urgently so as to avert the pending disaster, but Mr Duff informed him that he could only unlock them on receipt of written orders from the Navy and that until that happened he would

---

[*] See Chapter IV

[†] The sluice valves used to control water levels in the lock chamber.

do nothing. The City Surveyor dispatched an urgent note to the Admiralty at Portsmouth with the message *Kindly wire permission to open sluices to Mr Duff. It is imperative...* Duff was duly given orders to operate the paddles but the problem kept coming back, and when later that month the City Surveyor paid another visit to Birdham, he observed that the canal was overflowing above Casher lock. With no more ado he ordered his men to remove some of the stop planks on Casher lock and then rushed off to find Duff in order to get him to open the paddles at Saltern's lock to release the resultant bore into the sea. The City Surveyor was relieved to learn that Duff was prepared to do his bidding but as the water drained away another problem arose. Mr Vernon had a number of boats moored on the canal between the two locks, and one of these was tied so close to the bank that it tipped over as the water level dropped and it sank. It later emerged that the boat's rotten state contributed to its demise but that demise set the tone for the rest of the Admiralty's dealings with City Surveyor. On 2 February 1943, after the canal had overflowed again, the City Surveyor met the officer-in-charge at Birdham, Lt Stevens, who refused to lower the water again as he feared that more of Mr Vernon's boats would overturn. The Admiralty's Surveyor of Lands was then called from Bath* and he stated that it had not been the intention to requisition the whole of the canal, only its lower reaches, and therefore washed his hands over the fate of the banks above Casher lock. The City Surveyor pointed out that Mr Vernon had lost interest in the berthings as he had assumed that the Admiralty had taken them over and hence he could not be persuaded to adjust any moorings to allow the water level to be dropped. In a report to the Town Clerk, the frustrated City Surveyor expressed his concern about the safety of the banks of the canal saying *I have done everything possible to explain the seriousness of the position to the Admiralty...but at present [their] attitude appears to be that the canal belongs to the Corporation and it is the responsibility of the Corporation to deal with it and bear the cost of any damage to the banks of the canal*

* The Ministry of Defence had decamped from London to the comparative safety of Bath and requisitioned 2 Portland Place and the hideous (Victorian) Empire Hotel. They were still in *the Empire* in 1985!

The Admiralty, perhaps feeling a little vulnerable, revised their requisition on 28 February 1943 to release the canal beyond the moorings, but the flooding problems continued so the Town Clerk felt moved to write to them again to complain about their *inadequate handling of the problem* saying that the Corporation took a serious view of the matter *...and will be glad to learn that immediate action will be taken to deal with it.* The response to the letter was swift ; the first of many denying that the Admiralty had any responsibility for what had happened, and opining that the problems had arisen as a result of the poor structural condition of the canal in the portion not under requisition!

Mr Vernon's solicitors meanwhile pressed the Admiralty for compensation for the losses suffered by their client, and were offered £900, however the Corporation's dealings were not going so smoothly so they engaged the services of W O Stride to act as their land agent. Walter Stride ran a very successful practice from St John's Street, which is still in business today, and he accepted the commission and managed to get the Admiralty to attend a meeting in October 1944 to discuss a compensation claim. The Admiralty's position was still one of denied-responsibility. To mark VE day the Admiralty released all the requisitioned land* on 11 May 1945, with Chichester's canal fortunately not having been called to active service. It was then that the Corporation engaged the services of civil engineering consultants, Sir Cyril Kirkpatrick and Partners, to produce a report and estimates on the repair works needed to bring the locks back into a usable state, and also to negotiate with the Admiralty over getting the work done. In their comprehensive report Kirkpatricks detailed repair works estimated at £12,475 of which they opined that the Admiralty should pay £2,272 and the Corporation and Mr Vernon the rest. These recommendations were not well received in any quarters. The Admiralty felt that as the proposal to use steel gates classed as a betterment (it was!) they should not pay for it and therefore only offered £1,000 in full and final settlement. The Corporation meanwhile did not consider that

* All that is save for the club house which they continued to occupy – perhaps they preferred Birdham to Portsmouth.

they should pay anything at all since the lock had been leased to Mr Vernon on a full-repairing basis and it was thus his liability to make up for any past mismanagement. The debate rumbled on and it was not until 28 June 1947 that Strides finally managed to reach agreement with the Admiralty who would pay £1,688 plus a portion of Kirkpatrick's fee. The money was paid to Mr Vernon as tenant to put the work in hand.

Fig 13. Replacing the outer gates at Salterns Lock on 19 November 1955. The cab-less crawler crane was a real museum piece by then. (WSRO, Chichester Photographic Services archive)

Another change which occurred during the war was the removal of the superstructure of the Selsey Tramway bridge. When the railway closed in 1935 its assets had been sold by auction - mainly for scrap - but as the bridge across the canal was owned by the Corporation it was left in situ. In 1940 a pipe bridge at Shripney, which carried Bognor's water supply across a rife, was destroyed in a bombing raid so the main girders from the Selsey Tramway canal bridge were hastily removed to provide a temporary replacement[28] which survived until the early 1950s. Today only the mass-concrete abutment at Hunston remains as a reminder of this eccentric railway which has contributed so much to local folklore.

Peace returns

Responsibility for the canal had now been passed to the Corporation's Harbour Committee, and one of the first resolutions made about their new charge was to permit the City Surveyor to dump rubble from demolished air-raid shelters into the west end of the basin. Fortunately for posterity this plan was not carried into action, possibly because most Chichester people and institutions seemed to want to keep their air-raid shelters for storage purposes.

The water levels were kept up after the war and the Committee sought new leisure uses for the canal, including licensing the popular sport of angling* that was taking place from its banks. They agreed on 9 May 1948[29] to invest £500 in providing boating facilities - including the purchase of up to 30 boats - and advertisements were placed under a box number in *Yachting World* for the supply of suitable craft[30]. They were inundated with all sorts of offers and in October they advertised in *World's Fair* for tenders to operate the boats. Unfortunately this imaginative scheme was thwarted when the Corporation's application for a provisional order, to enable them provide hire-boats, issue fishing licences and supply refreshment, was refused by the Minister of Health.

In 1951 the Committee invested £615 a new weed-cutting launch to control the luxuriant growths that still occur in the waters, but

---

* In 1957 the City Surveyor reported that 80 or more anglers could be found at weekends

when in 1956 the 5th Chichester Rover Scout Group sought permission to canoe on the canal it was only granted *entirely at their own risk.*

The only one of the cast-iron swing bridges still in use was Poyntz bridge at Hunston and this was now beginning to feel its age. In 1954 Mr Reed, who farmed the land either side of the canal there, wrote to the Corporation offering to repair the bridge in concrete so that he could take his tractor and cattle across it in safety. The Harbour Committee agreed[31] subject to it being at Mr Reed's entire cost and risk and that he kept the public right of way open at all times. The impracticability of this caused Mr Reed to reconsider, and when the Committee refused to contribute towards the cost nothing more was done until 1956 when it was agreed to install a separate concrete footbridge. This was built, at a cost of £270, alongside the cast-iron superstructure which was then dedicated to Mr Reed's sole use.

Canal for Sale

In 1956 the Corporation had been considering the idea of selling the canal, and news of this reached the London Angling Society, and also the London and Provincial Angling Club, who quickly put in expressions of interest. This piscatorial interest should not be surprising as the canal had been popular with anglers since the late 19th century, indeed the etchings in figs 3 and 8 are taken from an 1890 angling magazine which was extolling its virtues.

The Committee resolved, on 17 September 1956,[32] to agree to the principle of a sale but needed to inform both the County and Rural District Councils first. They saw Clause 6 of the agreement with Westhampnett RDC, under which the highway authority could be forced to remove the culverts and restore the canal, as a positive benefit; a canal which could be made navigable to the sea should fetch a higher price than one which could not.

Another era in the canal's complicated history was drawing to a close.

References Chapter V

[1] WSRO Burrell MSS XXI/H/3
[2] WSRO Goodwood E3442 Conveyance
[3] WSRO Goodwood E2244
[4] WSRO C/18 Chichester Common Council minute book 1892-1894.
[5] Hadfield, Charles, The canals of South and South East England, 1969
[6] WSRO CA/9 Chichester Corporation Committee Minute Book 1896-1898
[7] WSRO CA/10 Chichester Corporation Committee Minute Book 1897-1900
[8] WSRO C/18 op cit
[9] WSRO CA/9 op cit
[10] Green, Alan H J *Hunston Canal Bridge,* Sussex Industrial History No 31, Sussex Industrial Archaeological Society, 2001
[11] WSRO CA/9 op cit
[11] Green, Alan H J, op cit
[13] WSRO CA/11 Chichester Corporation Committee Minute Book 1900-1902
[14] WSRO CA/10 op cit
[15] WSRO CA/15 Chichester Corporation Committee Minute Book 1910-1913
[16] Heneghan FD *The Chichester Canal* CP11 Chichester City Council 1958
[17] WRSO CA/13 Chichester Corporation Committee Minute Book 1904-1907
[18] WRSO CA/13 op cit
[19] WRSO WOC/CM5/1/19 WSCC Roads & bridges Committee minutes 1956-1958 cites this agreement
[20] ibid
[21] WSRO CA/21 Chichester Corporation Committee Minute Book 1927-1929
[22] *Chichester Observer* 14 October 1931
[23] WRSO catalogue entry for HC/9 Chichester Harbour Conservancy Records
[24] WSRO C/30 Chichester Common Council Minute Book 1937-1946
[24] WRSO HC/9/1/2/1 file of correspondence between the Town Clerk and the Admiralty
[26] Chichester Ship Canal Trust Newsletter winter 2004-2005 p6.
[27] WSRO HC/9/1/2/1 op cit
[28] Green, Alan H J op cit
[29] WSRO CQ/1 Chichester Corporation Harbour Committee minute book
[30] WRSO HC9/1/3 Files of Harbour Committee
[31] WRSO CQ/1 op cit
[32] ibid

CHAPTER VI

The Road to Revival 1957- 2004

Local politics

The Corporation, or Chichester City Council as they were now generally known, had good reason to wish to dispose of the canal. Their plans for reviving it for leisure purposes had been thwarted and the cost of its maintenance was proving a constant drain on its resources. In 1949 the expenditure[1] on maintenance, insurance, taxes etc came to £713-12s-1d, against an income from rents of £401-2s-6d. If someone else was prepared to take it on - and an offer of £5000[2] had been received – then this could only be to the ratepayers' benefit.

The news of the intended sale was met with some concern at County Hall; West Sussex County Council had had designs on using parts of the canal for road improvements (one of which would have filled up part of the basin) and loud alarm bells were ringing about that agreement with Westhampnett Rural District Council in respect of the culverts at Donnington and Birdham. As the County Council were now the highway authority, in succession to the erstwhile Westhampnett RDC, they had inherited the obligation under Clause 6 of the agreement to reinstate the canal should the need arise - an obligation which the canal's new owner might try to invoke. It was thought that this liability could involve public expenditure of up to £25,000 if the canal had to be reopened to navigation.

At the WSCC meeting on 18 April,[3] the County Clerk reported that he understood that the City Council were considering a *substantial offer* and so it was agreed to set up a sub-committee to *consider the matter and, if they found it necessary, to make a recommendation for the purchase of the canal by the County Council.* By purchasing the canal the County Council would become at once both parties to the agreement, thereby nullifying their obligation to restore the canal under Clause 6. They would also own the land needed for their intended road schemes. It is not surprising then that, at the meeting of 15 November 1957, the County Council voted to purchase the canal from the City Council for £7,500[4], a sum which included the weed-cutting launch. Solicitors then proceeded with the necessary conveyancing.

Another new broom

Despite the County Council's reasons for buying being far from altruistic from the canal's point of view, none of the road schemes, for which its land had been earmarked, came to fruition. As such no further losses of waterway were to take place and its new owner had to look for alternative uses. The principal one of these was still angling which became licensed and eventually the upper reach was leased to Chichester Canal Angler's Association. The stretch between Cutfield Bridge and Salterns Lock continued to be leased by the Chichester Yacht Company and between the two locks it became a haven for an eclectic flotilla of houseboats which, apart from the weed-cutting launch, were the only vessels to be seen on the canal until the 1980s.

During the 1950s and 1960s the area around the basin underwent dramatic change. The coal merchants moved out and Covers' timber yard, which had been sold to JH &FW Green in 1942, closed down in 1950[5] when the company relocated to the Hornet. Cover's yard was bought by the Southern Electricity Board who built new headquarters in Stockbridge Road and a social club (now Geoffrey Osborne's training school) overlooking the canal. Only the Covers' large family house still remains as a memorial to the site's former use. When the gasworks ceased production in 1958 the southern part of the site, plus the former canal company coal yards, was redeveloped as the GPO sorting office, which opened in 1964. As part of this development the canal house on the south-west corner of Basin Road - the twin to the custom house - was unfortunately destroyed.

The canal itself meanwhile was still slumbering, enjoyed only by swans, anglers and walkers albeit the latter had a hard time in the winter months as the tow path was not in a good state of repair.

Rebirth

The revival began in 1973 with the formation of the Sussex Canal Trust whose aim was to restore the whole of the Sussex line of the Portsmouth and Arundel Navigation. That first year the Trust restored a half-mile stretch of the abandoned main line at North Mundham, removing scores of trees from its bed and then refilling it with water, a project which had the full support of the local populace who welcomed the amenity of a waterway to their village[6]. Unfortunately by 1977 the Sussex Canal Trust had become dormant and so, on 16 May 1979, a meeting was held to revive the project by forming a new organisation with the same aims - the Portsmouth and Arundel Canal Society,[7].

In 1981 Brian Warner became the new landlord of the Richmond Arms and, being very keen to see the canal used, he began operating a small fleet of rowing boats from the pub. He also provided tables and seating on the edge of the basin and served food, so once again the Richmond Arms was providing refreshment for weary watermen, albeit the craft were somewhat different from those it served in the days of the Portsmouth and Arundel Navigation! Your author has happy memories of sitting outside *The Richmond* on a summer evening enjoying a pint under the close supervision of Brian's two enormous Great Danes.

The anglers were not to be displaced by all this and the two associations worked very closely together over the restoration project, with the Canal Society taking over the lease of the canal from the Angler's Association in 1984. The Canal Society began to dredge the silt, remove the weeds and rebuild the decaying tow paths for which they acquired a work boat which was craned into the basin in January 1982.

A popular feature of the 1980s was the annual beer barrel races held during the Chichester Festivities, organised by the Society in conjunction with the Richmond Arms. Teams competed for alcoholic prizes by rowing rafts made of lashed-together beer barrels up and down the basin. After Brian Warner's tragically-early death a trophy named after him was awarded to the overall winners. The beer barrel races attracted vast crowds of spectators, helping to make Cicestrians aware of this great asset they had on their doorstep.

In 1988 a black swan escaped from the Wildlife Park at Arundel and caused quite a stir when it took up residence on the basin, as did a goose with an identity crisis which, some ten years later, was adopted by a family of swans who treated it as one of its own.

Industrial Archaeology

The other organisation having a keen interest in the Portsmouth and Arundel Navigation is the Sussex Industrial Archaeology Society (SIAS), whose aim is to discover and conserve some of the lost engineering features of the Sussex line.

In 1982 the cast-iron superstructure of Poyntz Bridge gave up the ghost when the two centre girders broke as a result of excessive loading. West Sussex County Council rebuilt the bridge as a high-level fixed structure, using pre-stressed-concrete inverted 'T' beams on new concrete abutments. The old superstructure, rather than suffering the fate of all its brethren, was handed over to SIAS by the County Council as a restoration project, the intention being to re-site it on the abutments of Padwick bridge which were still intact. The old superstructure was craned out and taken to the Boys' High School playing field where it was analysed to enable a repair scheme to be devised. The restoration was the brain-child of the late Alan Alnutt, a retired chartered civil engineer,* who commissioned Chichester consulting engineers Sir Archibald Shaw and Partners to produce a design for replacing the broken central girders with new steel members. The physical work was all carried out by SIAS volunteers, and much external sponsorship was obtained, starting in 1982 with Carless Exploration Ltd† who donated £1,000[8]. Repair of the main structure was completed in 1986 when it was transferred onto stillages on the abutment of Padwick bridge, the crane being provided by Geoffrey Osbourne Ltd, the Chichester civil engineering contractor whose yard overlooked the basin. Work continued in

* For many years he chaired the Institution of Civil Engineers historic structures panel

† Carless were prospecting for oil in the Sussex Downs at this time.

replacing the missing set of parapet railings and the timber deck as well as shot-blasting and painting the ironwork, but the problem remained of finding replacement four-inch diameter balls for the pivot-bearing. Eventually a source was found in Sheffield, where F J Brindley and Sons still made hand-forged balls for use in cement-grinding mills and they generously supplied the 30 balls free of charge.[9] Sadly Alan Allnut was not to see the end results of his project and after his death completion of the work was led by Chris Bryan who also devised the method of, and carried out, the machining of the replacement bottom bearing ring in situ.

The bridge was officially opened by the Mayor of Chichester on 17 August 1997,[10] at a weekend event to mark the 175th anniversary of the (first) opening of the Portsmouth and Arundel Navigation. Unfortunately the weather proved somewhat inclement (well, it was August!) which had the inevitable effect on attendance, but it marked the completion of this important project and the bridge, which is always in operation on Heritage Open Days, remains in the care of SIAS.

Work has also been done by SIAS to clear and conserve the remains of the other swing bridges between Hunston and Salterns Lock but perhaps the most remarkable archaeological exploration has taken place between Ford and Hunston Junction. The twentieth century had not dealt too kindly with this section of the Sussex line; only three of the brick arches still remained in any state of completeness, part of the high embankment at Barnham had been removed, and much of the bed had been filled in and ploughed up.

Adge Roberts, who first became interested in the canal having spotted the *Canal Road* sign when driving through Yapton, began leading SIAS archaeological digs along the route in 2001. With the enthusiastic support of Bill Forse,* who owns Barnham Court Farm, the remains of Stewart Bridge were excavated, following which, by clever detective work, the positions of five of the seven swing bridges have been located and their remains unearthed together with Ford No 1 lock.

* Bill Forse has also excavated and cleared the section of the canal which crosses his land.

In 2004 these explorations embraced the new technology in using resistivity surveys, a process familiar to all *Time Team* fans, which reveals what remains below ground more easily than by digging. SIAS has erected public interpretation boards at sites of engineering interest along this route since the former tow-path remains a public right away despite the attempts by some landowners to obliterate it. Indeed in many places it is scarce possible to believe that there had ever been a canal there, which makes its eventual reconstruction something of a challenge.

Fig 14 The results of archaeological digs between Ford and Hunston. The site is that of Stewart (swing) Bridge at Barnham which has been excavated whilst the conserved iron main girder is from Hollinswoth bridge, the next structure along (Adge Roberts)

I must go down to the sea again…

In 1992 the Chichester Canal Society, as it had now become, moved a step closer to running passenger services with the purchase of a trip boat, a steel-hulled vessel that was fitted out by volunteers at the basin. It was appropriately named *Egremont,* becoming the fifth vessel in the Navigation's history to carry the name of its principal promoter. *Egremont* found another use as a floating bill-board during the flooding of Chichester in January 1994. That year Chichester reached national fame when the River Lavant burst its banks threatening to inundate the city centre, however, an extensive pumping operation, using *green goddess* fire engines, averted a major disaster. Much of the flood water was pumped into the canal whence it found its way to the sea. The councils and the Environment Agency then grappled with a means to avoid a repeat, and one option was to reopen the canal and equip it for the task. *Egremont* was moored in the centre of the basin and bedecked with a suitable banner campaigning for this option but, unfortunately, this wish was not to be granted. The final solution, only implemented after a second inundation in 2000, was to build an overflow channel into Pagham Harbour.

Fig 15 Egremont moored in the basin during the floods of 1994. Its message is obvious, but was not heeded. *(Author)*

In 2004 a second, larger, trip boat arrived, this time to be named *Richmond* echoing the noble name of the first vessel to be built at the basin in 1822 and at the time of writing is being fitted out. Meanwhile negotiations are in progress with the County Council about what to do with those culverts at Birdham and Donnington so that in the future this boat may, like the first *Richmond* whose launching John Marsh watched, make its way down to the sea.

The Portsmouth and Arundel Navigation has had a most challenging and interesting past and its future promises to be no less so.

****

References Chapter VI

[1] Chichester Corporation printed abstract of accounts year-ended 31 March 1949 (Author's collection)

[2] WRSO HC/9/1/4 Harbour Committee files

[3] WSRO WOC/CM5/1/19 WSCC Roads and Bridges Committee minute book 1956-1958.

[4] ibid

[5] Chichester District Museum, Trading Families in Chichester, u/p Lib 584

[6] Sussex Canal Trust newsletter January 1974 Adge Roberts collection

[7] Portsmouth & Arundel Canal Society newsletters – Chris Bryan collection

[8] *Chichester Observer* 20 May 1982

[9] *Chichester Observer* 20 October 1988

[10] *Chichester Observer* 21 August 1997

(1881)

(1923)

Endpiece. Advertisements for canal basin traders in Chichester Directories (Chichester District museum)

Suggestions for further reading

Canals:

Heneghan FD, The Chichester Canal, Chichester Paper 11, 1958
Vine PAL, London's lost route to the Sea, Middleton Press
Vine PAL, London to Portsmouth Waterway, Middleton Press 1994
Cuthbert, Ted, Portsmouth's Lost Canal, Portsmouth Urban Studies Association 1991.
Dashwood, JB, The Thames to the Solent by canal and sea, 1868 r/p Shepperton Swan 1980

Associated Chichester local history:

Foster, Paul (Ed), Marsh of Chichester 1752-1828, Otter Memorial Paper No 19 2004 (A collection of papers about John Marsh and his life in Chichester)
Green, Alan HJ, St John's Chapel and the New Town Chichester, Phillimore 2005. (for more information about Maj. Gen. Crosbie, William Dearling, John Marsh and James Elmes)
Griffith, Edward, The Selsey Tramways, EC Griffith 1974

Index

About Sussex Industrial Archaeology Society

Sussex Industrial Archaeology Society researches and records the working life of past generations through the physical and documentary evidence that they left, including how they travelled and the sources of power that were used. It encourages restoration of machinery, buildings and sites of industrial activity. Recent projects include Coultershaw Beam Pump near Petworth and a cast-iron swing bridge over the Chichester Branch of the Portsmouth and Arundel Navigation

The Society organises a series of winter lectures and summer visits. It produces a yearly journal, *Sussex Industrial History*, with definitive articles on the history of industry in the county; as well as a quarterly newsletter. Sussex Mills Group promotes the restoration and preservation of mills and milling and is part of the Society.

New members are always welcome, and information is available from the General Secretary R G Martin, 42 Falmer Avenue, Saltdean, Brighton Sussex, BN2 8FG

About the author

Alan Green was born in Chichester in 1950. Educated at Chichester High School for Boys he decided to follow a career in civil engineering which he did as a British Railways sponsored undergraduate at Portsmouth Polytechnic, whence he graduated in 1973.

He spent fourteen years in bridge design and construction and in 1987 he became the Project Civil Engineer for British Rail's works in connection with the Channel Tunnel project, which included the new International Terminal at Waterloo, the flyover at Stewarts Lane and the rehabilitation and electrification of the West London Line.

He moved to Railtrack in 1994 as Senior Contracts Manager for the South West Zone but left in 1997 to set up his own business in railway consultancy and also - fulfilling a long ambition - to write and lecture on his passions for Georgian and local history.

Researching and writing this book has enabled him to combine profession with passion!